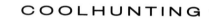

COOLHUNTING

Coolhunting

Chasing Down the Next Big Thing

PETER A. GLOOR

AND

SCOTT M. COOPER

AMACOM AMERICAN MANAGEMENT ASSOCIATION

New York · Atlanta · Brussels · Chicago · Mexico City · San Francisco
Shanghai · Tokyo · Toronto · Washington, D. C.

Special discounts on bulk quantities of AMACOM books are available to corporations, professional associations, and other organizations. For details, contact Special Sales Department, AMACOM, a division of American Management Association, 1601 Broadway, New York, NY 10019.
Tel.: 212-903-8316. Fax: 212-903-8083.
Web site: www. amacombooks.org

This publication is designed to provide accurate and authoritative information in regard to the subject matter covered. It is sold with the understanding that the publisher is not engaged in rendering legal, accounting, or other professional service. If legal advice or other expert assistance is required, the services of a competent professional person should be sought.

Gloor, Peter A. (Peter Andreas), 1961–
    Coolhunting : chasing down the next big thing / Peter Gloor & Scott Cooper.
        p. cm.
Includes bibliographical references and index.
ISBN-13: 978-0-8144-7386-3
ISBN-10: 0-8144-7386-5
    1. Creative ability in business. 2. Technological innovations—Management. 3. Social networks—Research. 4. Data mining. 5. Group decision making. I. Cooper, Scott (Scott M.) II. Title.

HD53.G55 2007
658.4'72—dc22

2006034160

Printing number
10 9 8 7 6 5 4 3 2 1

CONTENTS

In the summer of 2003, you could not walk into any twenty-something environment in San Francisco, where I lived, without hearing about Friendster—a new type of website, a *social network site*. You can't understand coolhunting without thinking about the importance of social networks (friends, family, coworkers, lovers). Likewise, it only makes sense to consider the rise in popularity of social network sites like Friendster and MySpace in order to understand coolhunting. Just like social networks allow people to spread ideas, social network sites allow people to leverage their social networks to spread information, culture, and gossip.

In this book, Peter Gloor and Scott Cooper explore what coolhunting is, describe many of its varied (and sometimes surprising) incarnations, and point the way to its practical application. The story of MySpace—the world's foremost social network site—illustrates both, while also explaining how broad and deep online coolhunting can be. To understand the rise of MySpace, however, we must begin with Friendster.

During that summer I mentioned, browsers on laptops in cafés were inevitably pointed at the Friendster site. Bands were talking it up on stage. And sitting around any bar or party, you'd be asked if you were on Friendster. The hype was everywhere, and people imagined that Friendster was going to be The Next Big Thing.

One of the most surprising things about Friendster was how far and how fast the news spread of the cool new site. Even before a single article about the site appeared anywhere in the mass media, more than 300,000 people had joined. As word spread, many participants lost track of the designer's original intention: to create a dating site. They saw Friendster as useful for so much more. By allowing people to create profiles and publicly display connections to others, Friendster provided a fantastic mechanism to support drama, social voyeurism, and the spreading of gossip. People tracked down old friends and stalked people they knew. To make the site more useful to them, users started creating profiles that would connect people based on shared interest or affiliation. These fake profiles (dubbed "Fakesters") proliferated as people started having fun with the site.

Of course, Fakester profiles were completely contrary to what Friendster wanted people to do on the site. The company began cracking down on users, punishing them by deleting their accounts when they acted out of line. While the company was trying to configure its users, their underlying architecture began to fail. At the same time, the company's desire for fame and popularity motivated them to bathe in the spotlight of the press. Although press coverage introduced new users, these users were disconnected from the core culture that had sprung up inside Friendster. Without being connected, the site was nearly useless to these newcomers.

Organic growth had been the key to Friendster's success—new users were socialized into the site from old users. The rush of newcomers was an additional signal to the active community members that they were not Friendster's top priority. Over time, the early adopters wandered away, disillusioned and abandoned by an environment they had once loved so dearly.

Sooner than expected, Friendster was passé, and coolhunters had a new place to search. What happened? How did this other social network site—MySpace—take its place as an icon of pop culture in the United States? And why on earth did Rupert Murdoch's News Corporation pay $580 million to own MySpace? The answers lie in the behavior of coolhunters, swarms, and the people who try to control them.

When MySpace launched to create a better version of Friendster, the early adopters were of a different breed. Because it was rooted in hipster Los Angeles, MySpace quickly attracted the indie rock community—including numerous indie rock bands that were kicked off Friendster. When they had tried to leverage Friendster to advertise their shows and their music, they were branded as Fakesters, and Friendster quickly squelched their participation.

MySpace recognized that they needed to let the cool people set the trend. When bands asked for special profiles, they got it. Because MySpace noticed that bands were telling people to go to their MySpace for promotional purposes, unique URLs were built that allowed fans to go directly to bands' profiles (and it certainly helped bands optimize search engines to find them). As a result, bands spread the word about MySpace. When younger people clamored to use the site, MySpace dropped the age limit: Teen culture flourished on MySpace.

MySpace could have demanded that their users behave in specific ways. Instead, they decided to watch the swarm and grow with it, to support the swarm in every way possible. Furthermore, their communication to users made it clear that they were trying to be helpful, not restrictive.

As will be discussed in *Coolhunting*, "memes" spread through social networks. (Richard Dawkins coined the term "meme" in 1976 to describe a unit of cultural information transferable from one mind to another.) And, in turn, these social networks allow coolhunters to track what is cool. Social network sites are inherently ripe for spreading ideas. Not only do social network sites allow people to model their actual social network, but they allow people to connect with people they think are simply cool or interesting.

Given the culture of MySpace, it is not uncommon for users to have thousands of "friends" on the system. These "friends" are not friends in the everyday sense, but rather anyone that individual users think are part of their cultural milieu. This includes friends, acquaintances, and anyone who seems cool or interesting. One incentive to connect to others is to see the posts on their bulletins, to hear what they think is important. Thus, the social networks modeled inside social network sites are magnified versions of the social networks that traditionally allow memes to spread. As a result, these sites support the rapid viral spread of anything the swarm feels is important—from fashion to music, social events to political protests.

Of course, social network sites don't just support users in spreading memes; they also support anyone who wants to hunt and track what's cool. In other words, pay attention to what people share—and what their friends share—and you can learn a lot about what is cool. What is the "in" TV show of the season? What band is hot? If people are into snowboarding, what else do they like? The information participants display on their social network site profiles is a marketer's dream.

It's hard to imagine that Rupert Murdoch was unaware of this quantity of valuable information when he purchased MySpace; no doubt Google saw this, too, when they promised MySpace $900 million to advertise on the site. Yet, while the big marketers can certainly scrape social network sites to follow what is cool, the publicness of this information makes it accessible to even the smallest of marketers and commercial enterprises. There are handbag artists who have profiles on MySpace and surf the site for people who might be interested in buying a handmade, personalized purse. Bands regularly reach out to fans of the bands that influenced them. Even politicians reach out to the young constituents that they think might hear their cause.

New tools are regularly emerging to support swarm activities, and one very visible aspect of these sites is an articulation of what is cool. It is easy to jump on social network sites and imagine new ways of selling products, but it is critical to keep in mind that the swarms are rightfully distrustful of those who try to regulate, control, or capitalize on their social interactions and identity displays.

Marketers certainly see social network sites as a way to leverage coolhunters, but most users see these sites as providing new ways to socialize. The flexibility of sites like MySpace allows swarms to innovate and find new ways of sharing cultural information. For most users, this innovation is not the primary goal, but it is a remnant of their attempts to repurpose the site to meet their needs. By being flexible and allowing swarms to remix culture, MySpace and other such sites provide a space for the development of cool.

In *Coolhunting*, Gloor and Cooper delve deeply into how these processes work. You will learn how swarm creativity can innovate and how it can go terribly wrong. You will learn how to make sense of trendsetters and how to track coolness in social environments. Through numerous examples and case studies, this book helps elucidate the culture of cool.

—danah boyd

ACKNOWLEDGMENTS

Any book project, except perhaps for those undertaken by the most reclusive of authors, involves far more people than the authors named on the cover. There are family members, friends, and colleagues who contribute in this or that way, sometimes directly by reading and reviewing and often indirectly by setting an example or inspiring an idea. Our list of people to acknowledge for their contributions includes people who fall into all of these categories.

Several professors at the MIT Sloan School of Management have, over many years, offered generous support and encouragement. Thomas J. Allen and Thomas W. Malone stand out—without their continuing help this book would not have been possible. We are also indebted to Hans Brechbuhl and Eric Johnson of the Center for Digital Strategies at Dartmouth College's Tuck School of Business for their invaluable support and for being constructive sounding boards.

Our thanks go as well to Wayne Yuhasz and Douglas Frosst; they were inspirational coolfarmers and role models, not to mention patient interviewees. Special thanks are due to Yan Zhao, lead developer of TeCFlow, and her husband Song Ye, who were always there to solve technical problems.

Detlef Schoder provided an invaluable review of the entire manuscript late in the writing process, and made some excellent suggestions that we incorporated into our work. Detlef, along with Maria Paasivaara, Caspar Lassenius, and Shosta Sulonen, also worked with Peter on the development of the course that provided an early testing field for our five steps of coolfarming presented in this book. Our special thanks go to the twenty-five students in the course at the University of Cologne and at Helsinki University of Technology, as well. In particular, we would like to give a special thanks to the following students: Paul Willems, Marius Cramer, Daniel Oster, Lutz Tegethoff, Sebastian Schiefer, Eero Uusitalo, Niko Schmitt, and Sebastian Niepel. Sung Jo Bae and Sebastian Schnorf did most of the work for the mobile-phone user study we present. Ornit Raz led the Israeli software startup research project. We are also grateful to Gary Shepherd for allowing us to quote his study on "The Family."

Francesca Grippa, Antonio Zilli, Giuseppina Passiante, and Angelo Corrallo from the University of Lecce in Italy were early testers of TeCFlow and verified many of the underlying social networking concepts. Christine Kohlert, Rob Laubacher, and Pascal Marmier provided invaluable feedback when we discussed many of our ideas. Richard Deutsch generously shared what he learned when creating the "Enhanced Gravity" multimedia CD. Adam Brown, who provided us with one of our finest examples from beyond the business world, was particularly inspiring.

We are grateful to Stan Wakefield, who played a key role in getting our book published with AMACOM, where editor Barry Richardson was very supportive and helpful. Thanks are due to Maya Mackowiak, who worked closely with us to review the manuscript and help ensure that we met the publisher's guidelines. Niels Buessem went above and beyond making necessary changes here and there, offering invaluable advice that resulted in making the book more reader-friendly.

Finally, we must thank our families. Scott's wife Jan read the manuscript and convinced us that the bees and beehive should be more at the center. Scott's children—Ben, Natalia, and Martha—always offer inspiration and were patient with the time devoted to the writing. Peter's children—Sarah and David—not only forgave their dad the weekends and evenings he spent in front of his Apple Powerbook, but also provided inspiration as exemplary coolfarmers and coolhunters.

Peter A. Gloor
Scott M. Cooper
Cambridge, Mass.
October 2006

COOLHUNTING

Introduction

STEVE JOBS and Bill Gates seem to know which inventions will become new trends. Warren Buffet has always had a knack for investing in stocks that become "hot." Toyota has created a cool trend with its highly successful Prius hybrid car, as has BMW with its Cooper Mini. And Apple has built a cult around its iPod. This book tells you how you can hunt for and predict cool new trends.

Since we began to think about coolhunting, a whole host of people have written about it. Noted author Malcolm Gladwell wrote about it in *The Tipping Point*,[1] and he talked about it in a PBS

"Frontline" documentary titled "The Merchants of Cool."[2] Websites about it proliferate.[3] Many claim—right and wrong—to know what it is. Others try to describe how it's done. No one shows you how to be a coolhunter and gives you the tools.

Is it coolhunting when the sneaker manufacturer finds the "coolest" kid at the skatepark, studies what he wears, and then uses that in his next design? A bit. Is it as simple as that kind of observation? Yes and no.

We've set out to show you what coolhunting is *really* about, and give you some ways in which you can become a coolhunter and even a coolfarmer (more about the farming aspect later). We put coolhunting as an activity on a systematic footing. You may think you know what coolhunting is, but we promise you that there's much more to it than meets the eye. It's not as simple as the simple description—*uncovering the source of trends*—often given. There's a lot more to it, not the least of which is to define what "cool" really means.

Lots of people are out there doing what they call "coolhunting." They're searching clubs for the girl who makes a fashion statement different from everyone else, and whose sense of style might be the "next big thing." They're looking for cutting-edge gadgets in unlikely places. But is that all coolhunting is really about?

No, it also concerns *how* groups of people work together to innovate.

New ideas can come from anywhere. So many of the best ideas come not from the individual inventor tinkering away in his garage, or even in a large corporate research laboratory, but from the collective efforts of groups of people. We see these groups of idea creators motivated by their love of the idea itself and by their devotion to a process of working with ideas that is predicated on nothing more than the great feeling that comes with success. They set out initially not with the thought of making millions (although this happens in plenty of cases), but to meet a challenge, solve a puzzle, and make the world a better place.

As we'll show you in this book, the coolest ideas often come from this collective mindset. "Swarm," for us, is an ideal word to describe that collective mindset, which unfolds as "swarm creativity"[4] within Collaborative Innovation Networks[5] (COINs, which we discuss throughout the chapters that follow). In biology, the term "swarm" is used to describe the behavior of a group of animals traveling in the same direction. We find the creativity unleashed by groups of human animals swarming together to be particularly compelling. So often, humans traveling together in the same creative, innovative direction produce the trends that are most interesting and exciting.

Slowly but surely, some business leaders are recognizing that the collective mind has a lot to offer when it comes to innovation. We see a promising trend: companies tapping into the swirling network of ideas around the globe that may not even correspond directly to the business the executives think they're in. They are seeing that innovation can come from the collaboration of people who share interests but not necessarily job descriptions, departments, disciplines, or other pigeonholes. They view an *expanded* collective mindset that reaches well beyond the walls of their offices and into every corner of the virtual world.

This is a welcome development, but there's a long way to go. More companies need to give up their closely held, internal innovation models and get out there and find what the *swarm* is creating. The innovation process will be served best when businesses realize that people motivated to collaborate and innovate because of shared interests, without specific regard for personal gain, create compelling new opportunities. This is the way to unleash the power of the innovation beehive.

Indeed, as we hope to convince you through this book, knowledge and innovation are often more valuable precisely because they are the product of the collective mindset. We define "cool" according to this very idea. The coolest—and thus most desirable—trends are the ones that feed off of this collectivity, this collaboration. In fact, the process through which innovation reaches great numbers of people is, itself, an example of swarm creativity at work. One example we offer in the book is that of the CEO of Continental Airlines coolhunting for trends in an online forum of frequent fliers. There are lots of other examples throughout.

Swarm creativity, in fact, creates some of the coolest trends for coolhunters to uncover. Google, Amazon, and eBay demonstrate just how rewarding it can be for businesses to employ swarm creativity—in which they give power away, share knowledge, and allow people to self-organize. How creative swarms behave as they collaborate can even be predictors of the future—often in rather counterintuitive ways. Who would have thought that the survivors of the dot-com bust in one country would have been the competitors who most shared during the height of the e-business craze? Knowing how to uncover this kind of information is what coolhunting is really about.

Our book is a guide for readers who want to employ the tools of coolhunting, including social network analysis and even an online software tool to which you'll have access. And we show you how to emulate some of the great coolhunters—and coolfarmers—of all time. Our role models come not only from the modern world of technological innovation, like the famous venture capitalist John Doerr, but also from hundreds of years ago. Old, stodgy Ben Franklin was, it turns out, one of the great ones.

It's one thing to talk about coolhunting. It's another to *do it*. With the right tools, and with a firm grasp of the axioms by which great innovations—ones that truly benefit us—can be coolhunted and coolfarmed, you *can* be a coolhunter.

1

Why "Cool" Matters

What I do is pattern recognition. I try to recognize a pattern before anyone else does.
—Cayce Pollard, in *Pattern Recognition* by William Gibson[1]

COOLHUNTING INVOLVES making observations and predictions as part of the search for cutting-edge trends. It is a way of capturing what the collective mind is thinking, and using what is captured to advantage. Tapping into the collective mind can offer tremendous benefits, and we will put these into the business context throughout this book.

Consider what Larry Kellner, CEO of Continental Airlines, did after participating in an online forum of frequent flyers.[2] Trendsetter Dean Burri, a Florida resident and Continental frequent flyer, was also online. Something about an issue he later couldn't recall prompted Burri to contact Kellner via e-mail. To his big surprise, Kellner responded twenty minutes later and the two of them ended up meeting.

Later, Burri helped arrange a meeting and dinner between Kellner and other frequent flyers to discuss how Continental could improve its services to become more attractive to frequent flyers. Invitations were offered on Flyertalk.com, a website devoted to discussion of travel industry "loyalty programs." Kellner thought fewer than fifty people would show up. Instead, close to 300 people traveled to Houston at their own expense (albeit for a visit that included several tours and a sumptuous meal) to talk with Kellner about the carrier's plans for the future and what they thought the airline should do to make customers happier. Getting their most loyal customers together—at customer expense—was a tremendous opportunity for the Continental executives to understand the needs of their passengers.

Burri describes the meeting as akin to an *Oprah* show, with the Continental frequent flyers asking tough questions about the disappearance of first-class seats, seat upgrade policy, and availability of "tickets for miles," and the Continental managers giving honest, straightforward answers. Although the frequent flyers did not like all the answers they got, they provided a unique sounding board for the Continental CEO and his team to learn first-hand about issues that mattered most to their most influential customers.

Larry Kellner is a great role model of a coolhunter. He is a savvy Internet citizen himself, listening to his most influential customer base on Flyertalk.com, and he is responsive and humble enough to answer an e-mail from a then unknown customer twenty minutes after he has received it in the middle of the night. He also demonstrated good judgment in contacting Burri, a trendsetter in the

Continental frequent flyer community who was able to convince 274 of his online "friends" to come to Houston. Kellner doesn't just listen, but he also takes action. Based on suggestions from the Flyertalk community, Continental has created a customer service desk dedicated to frequent flyers, has changed the format of its frequent flyer statements, and has improved its website to meet the specific needs of online bookers. Coolhunter Kellner is finding new trends by finding the trendsetters.

That's pretty cool.

What Is "Cool"?

Of course, if we're going to be talking about coolhunting, we need to start with a definition of "cool." Dictionary definitions (temperature considerations aside) include "not easily excited" and "not particularly friendly or sociable." The word "cool" became a positive epithet in English-language slang just after World War II, popularized by jazz musicians and meaning "excellent" or "superlative."

Today, the word means not only "excellent" but also suggests an element of being "fun" and even possessing a particular attitude—even in the case of inanimate objects (such as products). For example, many people consider Apple's iPod to be cool. The Volkswagen Beetle is cool. Snowboarding, the Web, Linux, Pokemon cards—all are considered cool, in some way.

The element of fun is definitely a part of our definition. Snowboarders have fun riding their boards. It's fun to surf the Web. Linux hackers really enjoy modifying and extending their Linux systems. For kids who collect Pokemon cards, Glurak, Shiggy, Pikachu, and Skaraborn are "way cool."

For our purposes, cool is about more than fun. To us, things that are cool make the world a better place, in some way. Coolhunting is about finding trends and trendsetters, and the trends we associate with cool make the world a better place. Take the iPod. How does it make the world a better place? We've all seen the advertisements, which show kids using iPods having a lot of fun. But look more closely. These kids are keeping out of trouble. They become responsible citizens—it's no accident that Bono, the singer from U2 and a touted social activist, is linked with the product. Who associates Microsoft-based MP3 players with being cool, even if they are technically superior to the iPod? Microsoft is feared (and admired by some) for steamrolling its competition, but when was the last time you heard anyone refer to anything about Microsoft as "cool"?

Google, on the other hand, is nearly always referred to as "cool." Perhaps Microsoft's most feared competitor, Google has made "don't be evil" its informal corporate motto.[3] Even more of a role model for coolhunting, Google is coolhunting for its own trends internally. Many of Google's innovations—AdSense, Google News, and Orkut, to name just a few—trace their origins to ideas generated by Google employees working on what the company calls "20 percent time." Google staff get one day off per week to come up with new ideas.[4]

Google's corporate motto ties in nicely with another aspect of what we think of as cool—altruism. We think of cool as having an altruistic component; it is cool to act for the benefit of others. Altruism is the view that others' well-being should have as much importance for us as does our own—and we find lots of examples where altruism, in a business context, pays dividends. In swarm creativity, altruism is essential. Selfless behavior propels great ideas forward.

We talk a lot about the bees in Chapter 2. But here, we want to make one great point about the bees with respect to altruism. We think it has important implications throughout the business examples we'll show in later chapters.

Bees defend their colonies to the point of sacrificing their own lives. When a bee stings you—which is always done as a defensive act—the stinger embeds in your skin and essentially anchors the bee to your body. When the bee flies away, the stinger stays embedded and pulls out the bee's soft internal organs—and results in the bee's death.

It's not that we advocate "dying for the cause," but we think this kind of altruism is not only very cool, but a powerful business strategy. You'll see how benefits can accrue through altruistic behavior in many of the business examples in this book, and we'll be talking much more about what is cool.

Coolhunting Offers Tremendous Benefits in Business

Coolhunting has many applications in all fields of business. In particular, there are two main application areas: watching external markets and unleashing internal innovation. The same principles can even be applied to forensic investigation.

Applying coolhunting to external markets, companies can detect new trends and trendsetters. This is of particular benefit to financial analysts, who can do in-depth analysis of market forces, consumer buying patterns, sentiment analysis, and market trends to make better-informed investment decisions. Capital management professionals, fund managers, and financial analysts obtain a 360-degree view of the markets they follow. Market analysts get nearly real-time insights into the relationships of people, ideas, and organizations. One financial analyst we know is using the TeCFlow software described in Chapter 7 to coolhunt blogs and find trends to report in his monthly investment trend newsletters. This helps him develop better investment research and advice for his clients. Trading house Cantor uses the Hollywood Stock Exchange, which it owns, to allow people to trade virtual shares in their favorite movies, actors, and musicians. While no real money is exchanged, Cantor mines the information generated on the market to predict entertainment success and popularity.

Market research professionals can discover new trends, who are setting those trends, and what knowledge is being shared across a given set of networks. A pharmaceutical company learned about the profiles of drug abusers, as well as more about drugs they abuse (and potential treatments) by tracking message board discussions. Continental CEO Larry Kellner learned about the latest trends in the flying business—including how select Continental flyers view what the competition is up to—as well as specific wishes of his frequent flyers. Providers of consumer products and services can identify lead users of new products and services as well as early adopters of products and services. MIT Professor Erich von Hippel found that new products proposed by end-users to 3M, the technology and chemicals conglomerate, produced eight times more sales revenue than new products exclusively developed by 3M's internal research and development organization.[5]

In another application of external coolhunting, venture capitalists can forego their conventional approaches and instead coolhunt for new investment opportunities by giving power away and letting future customers decide. Renowned venture capitalist John Doerr of Kleiner Perkins Caufield & Byers, whose spectacularly successful investments include Sun Microsystems, Lotus, Genentech, Netscape, and Amazon, coolhunts for new investment opportunities through swarm creativity in Collaborative Innovation Networks (or COINs), which we discuss extensively throughout this book. Doerr is legendary for his emphasis on the team. He asks not only for smart ideas and smart people, but demands passion and a shared vision—the main tenets of Collaborative Innovation Networks. He hunts the trends by looking for the trendsetters. Doerr acts as a connector—what we call a "galaxy" (a concept detailed later)—of executives from different startups in the sprawling ecosystem of Kleiner Perkins Caufield & Byers portfolio companies.

In the internal application of coolhunting, the same concepts can be used to unleash innovation within an organization to increase its performance, efficiency, and creativity. Executives can coolhunt within their organizations to uncover—and then support—new company-internal innovations in their early, nascent stages. Deloitte Consulting used coolhunting to identify trends and trendsetters among its own consultants to develop new service offerings for its clients (detailed in Chapter 4). Engineering giant Siemens has been using prediction markets—a form of coolhunting—to enhance its ability to set real deadlines and predict the success of its internal IT projects. Participants in the Siemens prediction market were particularly adept at anticipating new information about a software development project long before it was available through official sources. How? They integrate rumors and intuition into their prediction activity. In another application of company-internal coolhunting, Hewlett–Packard Laboratories uses prediction markets for sales forecasting, and has found that this type of coolhunting outperforms official Hewlett–Packard sales forecasts by orders of magnitude.

Coolhunting is not limited to discovering innovative new trends for common benefit, but can also be used for forensic investigations. The same coolhunting concepts can be applied to discovering "innovative" criminal creativity as to finding trends in the business world.

Coolhunting can benefit compliance analysts and members of the legal community. Intelligence analysis can track criminals, finding out who is writing to whom about what, when they are writing, and from where. In one of our research projects (discussed in detail in Chapter 6), we tracked the e-mail connections between the late Ken Lay, then chairman and CEO of Enron (later a convicted felon, only to have his conviction vacated after his death), and others at Enron convicted in the company debacle. Lay had claimed at trial to have known nothing of Enron's wrongdoings. While we cannot demonstrate direct e-mail interaction between Lay and Enron employees who had been convicted previously, we found dozens of gatekeepers connecting the delinquents to Lay, making it highly unlikely that he did not know of their wrongdoing. Looking at their discussions, we found them talking about highly suspicious topics, further weakening Ken Lay's claim of innocence.

Coolhunting extends into all domains of business life. Coolhunting principles can be applied by venture capitalists to discover new investment opportunities, by sales executives to create better sales forecasts, by project managers to enhance how software development goes, by financial analysts to identify market trends, and by marketing managers to predict consumer trends and trendsetters.

To understand better how all these people can profit from coolhunting, we need to understand how innovations spread and are accepted by user communities.

The Diffusion of Innovation

While research on how innovation spreads traces back to the beginning of the twentieth century, it really took off when two sociologists, Bryce Ryan and Neal Gross, published their now-famous study of farmers in Iowa.[6] Ryan and Gross classified the segments of Iowa farmers in relation to the amount of time it took them to adopt an innovation—hybrid corn seed. Academicians now call the process by which new ideas or products are accepted by groups of people the "diffusion of innovation"—a term coined by Everett Rogers, a professor at the University of New Mexico, in a now-classic 1962 textbook.[7] In his study, Rogers distinguishes between four steps in the diffusion process. First comes the innovation itself—the new idea that changes the lives of the people who apply the innovation. Next are the communication channels through which new ideas are disseminated. Rogers also looks at the time and rate of adoption of the innovation, seeking to establish criteria by which innovations spread out the fastest. Finally, Rogers explores how the social environment influences the way a new innovation spreads. Rogers studied first-hand the adoption of new agricultural technologies in his native Iowa, categorizing users into several categories, for which he also coined other new terms (perhaps his main claim to fame):

❏ *Innovators*—roughly the first 2.5 percent of users

❏ *Early Adopters*—the next 13.5 percent of users

❏ *Early Majority*—the next 34 percent of users

❏ *Late Majority*—the next 34 percent of users

❏ *Laggards*—the last 16 percent of users

Adoption and diffusion of new innovations follows an S-curve (Figure 1–1).

After slow initial acceptance of an innovation by innovators and early adopters, adoption reaches a tipping point, where usage explodes. It then levels off close after the early and late majority have

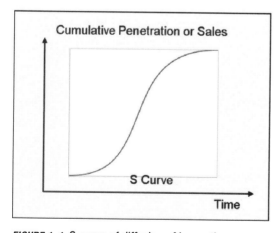

FIGURE 1–1. S-curve of diffusion of innovation. Source: Wikipedia.

adopted the innovation, with the laggards taking a disproportionate amount of time to finally adopt the innovation.

The researchers defined typical characteristics for the different types of adopters. The first farmers in Iowa to adopt hybrid seed, the *innovators*, were more "cosmopolitan"—they traveled more frequently to Des Moines and enjoyed a higher socioeconomic status than did later adopters. One of the most important characteristics of the first segment of a population to adopt an innovation is that they require a shorter adoption period than do people in any other category. Rogers identified several additional characteristics of innovators. They are more adventurous, with a desire for the rash, the daring, and the risky. They also control substantial financial resources to absorb possible loss from an unprofitable innovation. They have the ability to understand and apply complex technical knowledge, and also can cope with a high degree of uncertainty about an innovation.

Rogers also developed a profile of *early adopters*. They are an integrated part of the local society, and usually command the greatest degree of opinion leadership in the social system. They are respected by their peers, serve as role models for other members of their community, and are successful in their businesses.

Typically, *early majority* adopters interact frequently with peers, and they seldom hold positions of opinion leadership. They deliberate before adopting a new idea. The *late majority*, in contrast, adopts innovations only because of peer pressure and economic necessity. They are skeptical and cautious. *Laggards*, finally, possess no opinion leadership. They tend to be isolated, have the past as a point of reference, and are generally suspicious of the "new." Their innovation-decision process is lengthy and their resources are limited.

Everett Rogers breaks the adoption process down into five stages:

1. *Awareness:* "The individual is exposed to the innovation but lacks complete information about it."

2. *Interest:* "The individual becomes interested in the new idea and seeks additional information about it."

3. *Evaluation:* "The individual mentally applies the innovation to his present and anticipated future situation, and then decides whether or not to try it."

4. *Trial:* "The individual makes full use of the innovation."

5. *Adoption:* "The individual decides to continue the full use of the innovation."

Rogers also tries to understand why an innovator decides to *try* an innovation. Innovators proceed from their first knowledge of an innovation to forming an attitude about the innovation. They then progress to a decision—adopt or reject the innovation?—followed by implementation. The final step is to confirm the decision.

To come to the decision, innovators acquire three types of knowledge about the innovation. First, they need to become aware that the innovation exists. Then they need the information that will allow them to use the innovation properly. Finally, they need some knowledge of the underlying principles related to how the innovation works—what Rogers calls "principles knowledge."

The innovators form the principles knowledge. They are empowered to do so by employing the five external characteristics just described. People knowing about an innovation early on, have more formal education than later adopters. Early adopters of an innovation also have higher socioeconomic status and have more exposure to mass media channels of communication. They are also better connected socially and particularly well connected to other innovators.

They participate in more social activities and are more cosmopolitan than are later adopters. All of the above characteristics help them to develop the principles knowledge, which is then subsequently used by the majority to adapt the innovation.

To be fair, Rogers is not the last word on the diffusion of innovation. The actual rate at which an innovation is adopted is governed by both the rate at which it takes off *and* the rate of later growth. Some innovations that are relatively low-cost may take off quite rapidly; other innovations have a value that increases as adoption spreads and may experience faster growth at later stages. This latter phenomenon is called the "network effect"—which certainly corresponds to our concept of swarm creativity. Bob Metcalfe, founder of 3Com Corporation and co-inventor of Ethernet (a technology for local area networks), coined the term.

The network effect is a characteristic of an innovation that causes the good or service to increase in value to potential users based on an increasing number of users. The fax machine, which certainly was an innovation of significant consequence, is an ideal example. It was of no use to you if there wasn't a fax machine at the other end to which you could send your fax. The more fax machines there were out there—in other words, the greater the diffusion of the innovation—the greater was the value of the fax machine to any one user. The logic of the network effect is that as the value increases, so does the number of adopters.

The link between the network effect and swarm creativity is not simply the fact that growing numbers of people adopt an innovation, but also *how* the network effect plays out. Often, it is the result of word-of-mouth testimonials. One person sets the trend and passes it along to another, and the swarm grows. "The value of a network increases exponentially with the number of nodes," explains Bob Metcalfe in what has come to be known as "Metcalfe's Law."[8] E-mail is an ideal example of Metcalfe's Law. The more people you can connect via e-mail—that is, the more nodes in the network—the greater the value of e-mail to users (spam, of course, aside).

Further buttressing our view of the potential power of swarms is David P. Reed's assertion that Metcalfe's Law *understates* the value of adding connections.[9] When you connect to a whole network, particularly a social network, you also connect to many significant subnetworks. The existence of multiple opportunities for diffusion of an innovation among these subnetworks increases the value even faster than just counting up the individual nodes. This has been dubbed "Reed's Law."

Applying Rogers' theory, a successful coolhunter would look for people with the profile of innovators and early adopters and then follow them through the adoption process. Going further, a coolhunter might simply measure networks and try to find trends and trendsetters within those networks. But if it were so easy, wouldn't every marketing department have already figured it out?[10] Unfortunately, it is rarely so straightforward to discover and reach innovators and early adopters. Modern communication technologies, though, provide us with some new tools for the task—not only to reach these people, but even to discover and to track their communities. Dozens of years ago, some science fiction writers were already anticipating this development. What have we learned from them?

Predicting How Coolhunting Might Be Applied

Every technology geek knows that science fiction writers are often quite good at predicting new trends and technologies. For some thought-provoking scenarios about how coolhunting might play out in tomorrow's society, let's look at how three prominent science fiction authors forecast its use.

William Gibson's *Pattern Recognition* is set in a post-9/11 dot-com burnout world (mostly London) and tells the story of Cayce Pollard, a woman with psychological hypersensitivity that causes allergic reactions to brands and corporate logos. This trait makes Cayce Pollard the perfect coolhunter—the strength of her allergic reaction indicates the hipness of a logo or brand.

Cayce is part of a virtual community discussing the production and producers of a mysterious collection of video clips. The clips are published online, which is where the admirers hold their discussion in a forum. For the members of this community, finding the producers of the videos has become an obsession, supplanting basic needs for food and sleep. They form a tightly knit global community, displaying a kind of "brand loyalty" to these emerging bits of video footage. Cayce is hired to track down the producers of these bits of footage—after all, anyone who can generate products that inspire such tremendous brand loyalty would be a goldmine for Cayce's client. Cayce uses the online forum as her main means of pursuing the mysterious producers.

In the end, Cayce successfully tracks down the video producers, and also gets to know the real identities of her friends and enemies in the online community. In this sense, Cayce is a coolhunter role model, mining discussion patterns in online communities and blogs to discover the latest trends as well as the people who created those trends.

In this book, we want to teach you how you can become a Cayce Pollard. But we don't think you can rely on psychological hypersensitivity to discover trends. Coolhunting needs to be on a more systematic footing. Doyen science fiction writer Isaac Asimov painted a scenario that goes beyond intuitive coolhunting to take trend detection to the next level—trying to predict the future.

In his *Foundation Series*, Isaac Asimov describes how mathematician Hari Seldon develops a new science called "psychohistory,"

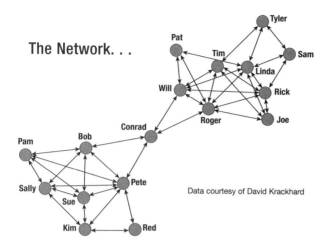

The Network. . .

Data courtesy of David Krackhard

FIGURE 1–2. *Sample social network.*

mixing elements of mathematics, statistics, and psychology as a way to predict the future based on the law of mass action. The basic premise is that while it is impossible to predict actions of the individual, actions of large groups of people—such as the populations of empires or even of entire planets—follow statistical laws. In Asimov's novels, Hari Seldon succeeds in predicting and steering the fate of humanity for an entire millennium, across the galaxy. To prevent a chaos of 30,000 years, Seldon establishes two foundations to build up a new and better world over a 1,000-year period—after which, the entire galaxy becomes one large self-organizing organism, *gaia*, collaborating in swarm creativity.

In this book, you will learn how to apply a much-simplified—yet tremendously powerful—form of psychohistory called "social network analysis." Social networks are relationships between groups of individuals, and they can be mapped. A typical social network picture is show in Figure 1–2.

The circles in Figure 1–2 represent people and the arrows between the circles represent relationships between the people—which can be family ties, seeking advice, working together, or any other type of relationship. The entire network picture is called a social network.

Two goals of social network analysis are to discover correlations between the positions of people in the social network and identify the characteristics, or properties, of individuals or the entire group. For example, there may be one person in the center of a network who controls the entire information flow and acts as a bottleneck by restricting information flow between the other members of the network. In Figure 1–2, Conrad is such a gatekeeper, and if he leaves the group it will break apart into two smaller groups.

In our own work, we have been able to discover social network group structures that are indicative of high performance or high creativity. We describe this later in the book, and show how social network analysis can be used for coolhunting and coolfarming. For now, suffice it to say that hunting successfully for trends through social network analysis requires knowledge about the social network structures. This is not necessarily an easy task, since individuals can be quite reluctant to report their relationships among each other.

Another science fiction writer, John Brunner, describes how to introduce transparency, particularly in electronic social networks. In his classic novel *The Shockwave Rider*, he describes what happens in a society where everyone is reduced to a code stored in the government's central computer, where the omniscient government collects all the details of each citizen's life history. It takes rebel computer hacker Nick Haflinger, groomed by the government to be part of the knowledge elite, to introduce transparency into this wired world. A super-programmer, Nick is able to create new identities for himself by breaking into the government computer. By introducing total transparency and exposing the corruption of the government online, Haflinger succeeds in creating a newer, better society in which everyone is equal and in which gets access to everyone else's information.

Our approach to coolhunting combines Asimov's basic ideas about the predictability of social interaction patterns of large groups with Brunner's concept of transparency in a wired world, and then applies it to Gibson's coolhunting concept. His coolhunter, Cayce Pollard, is a hypersensitive human, but we're trying to augment human coolhunters with automated communication pattern analysis similar to Asimov's psychohistory.

Shockwave rider Nick Haflinger resembles Cayce Pollard in that he is more sensitive to emerging trends than the rest of the world. He uses his hypersensitivity to introduce total transparency, similar to the basic principles of COINs and swarm creativity. Collaborative Innovation Networks flourish because the contributions of every COIN member are obvious to the community, and each person is rewarded in a meritocratic way through peer recognition. This is similar to the gargantuan roadmap for humankind set out by Isaac Asimov, who outlined a future where mass actions can be precalculated and an *Endzeit* scenario where human innovation converges in one meritocratic organism for the greater good of the universe.

In the chapters that follow, you'll meet real-life coolhunters and see how swarm creativity works in Collaborative Innovation Networks. We'll show you how you, too, can be a coolhunter. Let's begin by looking at how swarm creativity creates cool trends.

2

Swarm Creativity
Creates Cool Trends

While Linux has been my baby so far, I don't want to stand in the way if people want to make something better of it.
                    —Linus Torvalds, creator of the Linux operating system[1]

HUMANS SWARM around like-minded people, with whom they not only feel comfortable but also can collaborate to produce winning ideas. With the advent and expansion of the Internet in recent years, they have gotten an immense boost, and can form instantaneously and collaborate on innovative tasks from almost anywhere on the planet as Collaborative Innovation Networks. COINs are cyberteams of self-motivated people with a collective vision, enabled by technology to collaborate in achieving a common goal—an *innovation*—by sharing ideas, information, and work. Working this way is a key to successful innovation. If a COIN innovates around a trend identified through coolhunting, it is highly likely that the end result will be at the cutting edge of where the collective mind *wants* to be taken. To phrase it differently, to find the cool trends we need to look for COINs working together in swarm creativity.

To understand better how swarm creativity and the collective mind works, let's look at how social animals self-organize.

Self-Organization in the Beehive

People working together in swarm creativity exhibit many parallels with beehives, and the best swarm creativity is that which most closely replicates the behavior of bees.

Day-to-day activities in the beehive are coordinated directly among the self-organizing worker bees, with no intervention by the queen. She is constantly attended to and fed royal jelly by the colony's worker bees. The number of eggs she lays, though, depends on the amount of food she receives and the size of the workforce capable of caring for the brood. She has no direct way of influencing the quality of the work performed by the worker bees, even though the quality of her own work is strongly influenced by what the worker bees do.

In a COIN, members also self-organize to coordinate their daily tasks. One striking parallel between beehives and COINs is what happens when leaders "fail." When members of a COIN are no longer happy with their leaders, they democratically choose whomever is "best suited" for succession. A similar process unfolds in the beehive when an old queen becomes unable to fulfill her duties.

Queens develop from fertilized eggs or from young worker larvae no more than three days old. New queens are raised if any of three different impulses occur in the hive: emergency, planned succession, or swarming. When an older queen begins to "fail" by laying fewer eggs than in the past, the colony prepares to raise a new queen. Bees select their new queen in swarm creativity: the rank-and-file bees decide who their future leader will be, not the queen. The bees feeding the larvae—and not the queen laying a special egg—decide whether to feed special food to chosen larvae in the brood comb. Whereas in the beginning all larvae are equal and all are fed the royal jelly, after three days only the chosen larva continues to receive the royal jelly. The others, who will be worker bees, are switched to ordinary food. When a queen is accidentally killed or removed by the beekeeper, the bees can also select older worker larvae to produce emergency queens. Queens produced under an "official succession plan" usually perform better than do emergency queens, since they are fed larger quantities of royal jelly during their development.

There are strong parallels between the bees feeding a new queen "royal jelly" and new members in a COIN being "fed" knowledge by their peers in the COIN. The better the bees are at feeding the "royal jelly" to their future queen, the better she will perform. And the same is certainly true for COINs: the better senior COIN members are at sharing their knowledge with new COIN members, the better able the new members will be at collaborating with established COIN members and the better the entire swarm will perform. There are even parallels to the selection of human leaders, who usually perform better if they get the opportunity to learn the tools of their trade from the bottom up. And sometimes leaders of COINs are removed by external events, like the beekeeper removing a queen bee.

In yet another swarm impulse, new queens are produced in preparation for swarming. Swarming occurs when the population of a beehive has grown enough to split into two and send off a new swarm. This is different from ordinary succession planning, where an old queen has simply grown too old and ineffective to deliver adequate service to her hive. In the case of swarming, the new queen and one half of the bees stays in the old hive, while the old but still healthy queen takes the other half of the bees and leaves in search of a new location to set up a new beehive. Collaborative Innovation Networks do the same thing: they continuously redefine their memberships, and are ready to split if a sizable group of the old swarm wants to pursue new directions.

The old queen bee and the newly raised princess may both be present in the hive for some time. Once the young queen has matured, the old queen creates space for the new one, and leaves the beehive with half her population to start a new beehive.

From an unlikely source—the writings of the Dalai Lama—we find a good case made for what the bees offer as a model:

> When I consider the lack of cooperation in human society, I can only conclude that it stems from ignorance of our interdependent nature. I am often moved by the example of small insects, such as bees. The laws of nature dictate that bees work together in order to survive. As a result, they possess an instinctive sense of social responsibility. They have no constitution, laws, police, religion or moral training, but because of their nature they labour faithfully together. Occasionally they may fight, but in general the whole colony survives on the basis of cooperation. Human beings, on the other hand, have constitutions, vast legal systems and police forces; we have religion, remarkable intelligence and a heart with great capacity to love. But despite our many extraordinary qualities, in actual practice we lag behind those small insects; in some ways, I feel we are poorer than the bees.[2]

The behavior of bees illustrates one of our principles of swarm creativity: Give power away to gain power. We quote the Dalai Lama not only for his concise description of bee behavior, but also for his notable last point—that "we are poorer than the bees." Why shouldn't we enrich ourselves in the way of the bees—who gain power for the collective good by giving power away within the swarm?

We will return to the bees several times in later chapters. For now, let's concentrate on this one principle.

It's Cool to Give Power Away

In Chapter 1, we discussed the altruism of the bees. It is a concept closely linked to the notion of giving power away.

Arnold von Winkelried is a legendary (and probably apocryphal) hero in Swiss history (more on Switzerland later in this chapter). He was, for all intents and purposes, a bee. In 1386, when his Swiss compatriots were facing the army of Leopold III of Austria at the battle of Sempach, Winkelried is reputed to have made it possible—*single-handedly*—for the Swiss to emerge victorious.

The story is that the Swiss forces could not break the lines of the Austrian foot soldiers. According to the legend, Winkelried had a plan for breaching their ranks. Allegedly, he cried: "I will open a passage into the line; protect, dear countrymen and confederates, my wife and children." He then threw himself against as many of the Austrians' lances as he could, which knocked over the soldiers. The Swiss attacked through the opening—and won the day.

The story of Winkelried is an allegory for a very simple idea: that success often depends on sacrifice. The sacrifice we wish to discuss is not one's life, but power.

THE EXAMPLE OF COSTA RICA

Leaders who give away power can unleash immense energies for the common good. Take the nation of Costa Rica. It became the most prosperous country in Central America precisely by giving power away. In 1949, President José Figueres Ferrer abolished the army, and ever since Costa Rica has been one of the few countries in the world to operate a democratic system of government with absolutely no military. Abolishing the army has prevented a military group from gaining autonomy and power—which has been a problem in many Latin American countries. Without an army, the only route to power in Costa Rica is through elections. The public funds absorbed by military spending can be used by Costa Rica for social welfare and development.

Costa Rica's investments have paid off. The country has social security and health-care systems equal to or better than many industrialized nations. In sharp contrast to much of Latin America, even the country's smallest towns have a right to—and receive—electricity, public and private telephone service, and potable water. More than one-quarter of all Costa Rican territory is set aside for national parks, biological reserves, forest reserves and buffer zones, wildlife refuges, and Indian reserves. And Costa Rica has more teachers than it does police.

THE EXAMPLE OF SWITZERLAND

Costa Rica is not the only country that has been highly successful by giving power away. Switzerland is a prime example of how giving power away benefits an entire nation. Back in 1291, three cantons (or states) of modern-day Switzerland decided they no longer wanted to suffer the aggression of surrounding cantons or endure foreign rule. They established the "Everlasting League"—which later became the Swiss Federation—and declared in their charter letter "a single nation of brethren" (*ein einig Volk von Bruedern*) in which all would be equal. Over the next few hundred years, Swiss farmers repeatedly beat back huge armies of foreign invaders. Carried away by their own success at this, the Swiss themselves began conquering large stretches of Europe, both north and south of Switzerland's own territory. But in

1515, in the battle of Marignano in northern Italy, the French and Austrians decisively beat the Swiss. Switzerland learned some valuable lessons—which formed the basis for the nation's declaration of "neutrality." With a few exception, the Swiss have stayed neutral ever since.

Switzerland was the only country of Europe that did not fight in World War I or World War II—although the Swiss certainly have defense forces. The Swiss army is an institution deeply anchored in the public, based on the military defense successes of the last 700 years. Every male Swiss citizen must serve in the army, and is given an automatic rifle and ammunition to take home. Switzerland gives *armed* power away. Even though every Swiss home has a loaded rifle, Switzerland enjoys a very low crime rate.

The Swiss also have one of the most democratic states in the world. All decision-making power is delegated to the people. There is neither president nor prime minister; instead, seven people serve as Federal Councilors. They are not unlike the average Swiss person—it's typical for Federal Councilors to take the bus or train to work, and they travel without bodyguards.

All major decisions in Switzerland—ranging from national issues such as whether to join the United Nations or the European Community to regional questions such as which lands should be converted to national parks, community tax hikes, or the building of new soccer stadiums—are taken by public vote. Every legislative decision is subject to a referendum. If a group of citizens disagrees with a decision of the lawmakers, they can collect signatures and request a public vote. Switzerland gives power away to the swarm.

Just how successful has Switzerland been giving power away to its citizens? For the last 30 years, Switzerland has been one of the world's wealthiest countries—and the wealth is widely shared. For example, Swiss citizens are considered below the poverty line if they make less than $25,000 per year, but the Swiss nation increased that income to a point above the line through subsidies. Switzerland has only about 2 percent of Europe's population, but is home to three of Europe's ten largest companies (Nestlé, UBS, and Novartis) and hosts many more Fortune 500 firms. The country is also among the world's most innovative. Statistics of the World Intellectual Property Organization rank Switzerland as having the highest per-capita rate of patent filings of any country.[3]

ONLINE COMPANIES

Giving power away truly leads to swarm creativity, as the Swiss example shows. It has paid off nicely not only for countries but even more so for companies—Internet firms in particular.

Google became one of the fastest-growing, most profitable companies in a very short time by giving away its core product—its powerful search engine—free for the asking. Meanwhile, Google continues to expand that product to include other programs and services such as e-mail, instant messaging, and even Internet telephony. The company makes its money mostly from advertising on its site, and the site is a highly desirable place to advertise because of the number of people attracted to Google.

Both eBay and Amazon succeed by turning decision-making power—and the decisive components of the buy/sell process—over to their users. Sales at Amazon are driven in large part by the simple recommendation system, which is based on buying patterns of customers and by making common interests among buyers transparent. eBay functions as a matchmaker, having outsourced the entire buy/sell process to users. Its users even have the power to establish or destroy the reputation of all vendors and buyers.

Skype, a software application that allows people to talk and instant message for free via their computers, gives away a kind of power—its product. The company first generated revenue by selling value-added services to users, such as voice mail and the ability to phone someone using a regular phone, via Skype, for a fee much lower than that charged by the phone companies. Eventually, Skype leveraged giving itself away into a multi-*billion* dollar buyout by eBay, which plans to combine its core product, its PayPal online payment system, and Skype into what eBay CEO Meg Whitman has called a "power trio" that will deliver an "unparalleled e-commerce and communications engine" by "removing a key point of friction between buyers and sellers."[4]

THE VIRTUAL LABORATORY

One of the more compelling examples of the power of giving power away comes from the world of scientific research. It challenges the traditional model of research and development held close to the vest, locked away in a tightly controlled laboratory under one company's umbrella. Instead of the Bell Laboratories of old, or a "skunk works," we find the model of a matchmaker between researchers and those who seek the fruits of that research to commercialize.

In July 2001, Eli Lilly and Company—one of the world's leading pharmaceutical firms—incubated a startup business venture through its e-business division. Lilly was looking for a way to expand its access to chemists while also exploring how it might shift the financial risk associated with pharmaceutical research and development.[5] InnoCentive became the solution. InnoCentive links researchers together in what it claims to be the "world's largest virtual laboratory."[6] There are more than 90,000 scientists, researchers, engineers, students, and others in 175 countries registered on the site.

Lilly was the first company to use InnoCentive's services. Since then, InnoCentive has become independent and Lilly is one of many companies in the sciences—now including not only chemistry, but also biology, biochemistry, and materials science—that find collaborators in this way. "It has signed up more than 30 blue-chip companies, including Procter & Gamble, Boeing, and DuPont, whose research labs are groaning under the weight of unsolved problems and unfinished projects."[7]

Companies that enter into a contractual relationship with InnoCentive are called "Seekers," and they can post what the company calls "R&D Challenges." People who register are called "Solvers"—they review the challenges and can submit solutions online. Seekers then review what the Solvers offer and select what they consider to be the best solutions. InnoCentive awards the Solver with the financial incentive established by the Seeker; these incentives range from $10,000 to $100,000.

The financial incentives, though, are only part of the picture. Solvers get the intellectual challenge that comes with working on R&D problems that match their interests and expertise, recognition for their skills and talent, *and* the financial reward if they solve the problem. A look at award winners on the website reveals that while most are academic- or research-company-based scientists and engineers, some are working on these problems while spending time in other walks of life. A recent award-winning Solver for breast cancer risk assessment, for instance, operates a garden center and landscape business with his wife.

One of the rationales behind InnoCentive and similar ventures that have since appeared is the notion of "democracy." Ali Hussein, InnoCentive's vice president of marketing, explains it as a way to "insource" for R&D talent by:

> . . . leverag[ing] the democratizing force of the Internet to reach some of the top scientific minds in the world. . . . Using the Internet to exchange knowledge is the next logical step in its evolution. . . . Trading on intellectual capital and scientific

knowledge is a business waiting to happen. You never know where a solution can come from, and sometimes, it can come from the least likely of individuals.[8]

Alpheus Bingham, now InnoCentive's president and CEO, also uses the democracy metaphor. "We are talking about the democratization of science.... What happens when you open your company to thousands and thousands of minds, each of them with a totally different set of life experiences?"[9]

The $9 million infusion of venture capital InnoCentive received in February 2006 is an investment in swarm creativity, intelligence, and giving power away to gain power. "There is a 'collective mind' out there.... The question is, what fraction of it can you access?"[10]

These are but a few examples. Giving power away is itself powerful, as Open Source leaders have learned. Linus Torvalds gets it, and has put this principle to work with the Linux operating system he invented. Linux is available free to anyone who wants it. Torvalds has delegated decision-making power and there is a completely transparent and meritocratic "promotion" process for the ideas that Linux developers come up with. Having given away power, Torvalds has an absolute grasp on the development process of this technology.

It's Cool to Share Knowledge

Linus Torvalds didn't just give away power with Linux. The entire idea of Open Source software is that it's cool to share knowledge. Members of Open Source development teams list as their main motivation for participation the desire to learn cool new technologies and getting to know cool new people. Besides getting to know new stuff and making new friends, sharing knowledge can also have huge tangible benefits. It's not just in the beehive, where feeding enough "royal jelly" to the future queen benefits the entire swarm by nurturing a strong queen. In the COIN as well, when senior members feed knowledge to new members it benefits the entire Collaborative Innovation Network.

Consider the case of thirteen research laboratories from ten countries collaborating to discover the causes of the SARS disease.[11] Through the World Health Organization's Global Outbreak Alert and Response Network (GOARN), scientists, clinicians, and epidemiologists were linked during the period of outbreak containment in virtual networks that allowed them to share knowledge openly and quickly about the causative agent, mode of transmission, and other features of the disease. This real-time information made it possible for the World Health Organization to guide health workers in the affected countries on how to manage the epidemic and take protective measures to prevent further spread of the disease. By working together with those thirteen labs, pharmaceutical giants Pfizer, Merck, Bristol Meyers Squibb, and Novartis were able to develop new drugs that none of them would have been able to develop on their own.[12]

Sharing knowledge can even be lifesaving in times of crisis, and collaboration and swarm creativity can be powerful forces for good. This is clear from new collaboration in cancer research.

Some fifty cancer centers across the United States agreed to join a Cancer Biomedical Informatics Grid that Ken Buetow, who directs the National Cancer Institute Center for Bioinformatics, calls a metaphor for "semantically interoperable World Wide Web of cancer research."[13] It will function as a bioinformatics resource center filled with data about specific pathogens.

Bioinformatics, broadly defined, is the application of computer technology and information science to collect, organize, interpret, and predict biological function and structure. It is a rapidly growing scientific field, spurred by the worldwide interest in the human genome and analyzing DNA sequence data. Bioinformatics itself is an example of swarm creativity; experts in three disciplines—biology, statistics, and computer science—swarmed together over a period of some years to create a single discipline.

The Cancer Biomedical Informatics Grid is a good example of collaborative innovation, based on swarm creativity, where the expected payoff from increasing collaboration is better research, easier and more effective clinical trials, and—eventually—usable treatments for a killer disease. It will correct a longstanding problem that has plagued university researchers, cancer centers, and other organizations: the absence of a cohesive way to collect and share data.

Robin Portman of Booz Allen Hamilton, one of the contractors working on the project, explains that creating this grid—which we think has the potential to be a very successful COIN—will promote a common infrastructure and allow the research community to "focus more on innovation."[14] One of the best indications that a COIN is on the horizon: the initial developers expect ownership and future development of the grid, once established, to be taken over by the research community itself.

The National Cancer Institute will make raw cancer research data available on the informatics grid, which will allow participating cancer centers the opportunity to do data mining that can assist their specific research programs. Eventually, the grid will be made accessible to the Food and Drug Administration and even pharmaceutical companies.

How cool would it be to wipe out the scourge of cancer thanks to a Collaborative Innovation Network?

It's Cool to Self-Organize

One of the authors happened to be in London in 2005 when the bombs went off on the city's rapid transit system. Peter was on his way back from an academic conference in Greenwich, traveling across the city to a research meeting. When he left the Greenwich train at London Bridge to catch the Thameslink train that would take him to the meeting, there was no connecting train. The first bombs had already gone off, and more would follow.

Announcements were being made that the city was about to be closed to all traffic, and everyone was asked to head home, but no one really knew what was happening. The station was overflowing with people waiting to get on their trains back home. People only knew that the Tube wasn't working.

Peter was finally able to take a train to Bedford, which traveled slowly beneath the city. The train, full of people, stopped at King's Cross, but no one was allowed to get off. People had mobile phones and were trying to call friends and family to let them know they were okay and to ask what was going on. But the mobile phone network was so congested that communication was painful. When people did get through, they would share whatever news they had across the car.

It was impossible for Peter to reach by phone the people who were expecting him at the meeting. Finally, he got a long text message from his daughter in Switzerland, who told him what was going on. He immediately shared this news with the people close by, who shared whatever bits and pieces of information they had gotten. Slowly, everyone in the car learned what was happening above ground and elsewhere in the tunnels. As more news came in, the picture became increasingly dark—but, amazingly, no one panicked.

People in the London Tube were self-organizing in calm determination that day. Evacuations went smoothly. Those trapped in trains shared information and calmed each other's nerves. This is swarm creativity at its best, overcoming evil. Swarm creativity and self organization can also be put to productive use to make our world a better place.

The World Economic Forum (WEF) held each year in Davos, Switzerland provides a simple but compelling example of how collaboration can lead to ideas—but one of the best examples is not the aspect of the Forum you might imagine. Yes, the rich and mighty convene to discuss the state of the world. And yes, official sessions focus on environmental protection, Palestine and Israel, and other grave topics. But one of the main reasons CEOs, state ministers, and others like to come to Davos is for the informal networking. Nowhere are there so many heads of state, leaders of Fortune 500 companies, and celebrities in the same place at the same time. Organizers are well aware of this, and offer numerous social events and gatherings to give people opportunities to mix, mingle, and network.

In addition to all the rich and famous, many of the participants at the WEF attend simply because they care. From the members of a youth group working on building bridges between Protestants and Catholics in Northern Ireland to the representatives of self-help women organizations in black Africa, they have been chosen by the Davos organizers to represent their causes at the Forum. They are the real trendsetters, leaders in their communities, who become plugged into the global network of the powerful at the WEF.

Peter remembers a discussion he had a few years ago with a colleague at work, who was an active member of that Northern Ireland youth group. He spoke of the unique opportunities he had in Davos to connect and network with both his "adversaries turned partners" and potential relationship brokers, and of the lasting relationships he forged in Davos to help meet his goals.

Many participants will tell you that the best things about Davos are not the official gatherings, where the "best" discussions are supposed to happen. No—the best things about Davos are the little buses that circulate around the small city all day, shuttling participants from one event and one hotel to the next. The seating in the buses is arranged to encourage discussion, and passengers never know what interesting people they might encounter. From the U.S. intellectual who has converted to Islam, to a manager from a Swedish company leading the way in some innovation, to a Kenyan marathon runner—it's possible to encounter people from all walks of life. The buses are an ideal opportunity to meet people from beyond your own sphere, network, and share ideas. This is where the "unofficial" trendsetters such as Peter's colleague get their chance to meet the mighty and powerful, to self-organize in swarm creativity, and to build their network of trendsetters—connecting previously disparate geographical and social spheres.

Let's now see how swarm creativity can be applied to coolhunting.

Applying Swarm Creativity to Coolhunting

The story of the Worlddidac jury shows that there are *professional* coolhunters in the real world. The jury is a group of education experts who have been getting together periodically over the last twenty years to identify the most innovative products in the education market. They look for products that will have a real impact and be hugely successful. Every other year, the jury gives out Worlddidac awards for these products. The awards are sponsored by the Worlddidac Foundation, the global nonprofit association of educational materials producers.

Put simply, the jury is coolhunting, looking for the coolest education products. Of the plethora of new products, the jury must decide which are the ones that will "change the world." The selection process happens in two steps: First, there is the Worlddidac secretariat, whose members have an excellent grasp on new developments in the realm of educational products. If they find a new product they think is truly innovative, they encourage its producer to submit it to the Worlddidac award. Additionally, producers can also directly submit their products to be judged. In this sense, the Worlddidac award process combines coolhunting by the Worlddidac secretariat with self-organization by the entire community of educational material producers.

The Worlddidac awards jury derives its authority from the fact that its members are considered the "best and brightest" experts in their fields, recognized around the world. Rarely are any of the jury's decisions questioned by the people who submit products. It has an enviable track record over two decades of picking scores of future winners: the first Lego technical bricks, overhead projectors, video cameras, some of the best-selling educational music CDs, schoolbooks, and interactive Web-based training programs are among the award recipients.

Most amazing is that the jury does its coolhunting based on swarm creativity.

For the last ten years, Peter has served on this jury with six to seven other experts, and has chaired the group for the past six years. They get together every second year for three days somewhere in Switzerland to look at presentations of the latest and greatest in educational products. Each time, some fifty to eighty products are nominated, and they have the challenging task of finding the dozen or so outstanding products that are truly innovative and that they think will have a deep impact on students. Past submissions have ranged from models of human skeletons, to preschool toys and kindergarten furniture, to entire greenhouse chambers the size of a room, to chemistry kits sturdy and affordable enough for the most remote classroom in Africa. Most products are represented by their creators, who fly in from throughout the world to give a 20-minute pitch. This is an opportunity for the jury to be inspired through experimentation, by learning new things, and by gaining fascinating insights into the most creative solutions for teaching new skills to students anywhere on the planet.

The Worlddidac secretariat has become highly skilled in selecting suitable candidates for the jury, and the jury has developed a sophisticated decision-making process since the awards were first launched. It makes the evaluations as fair and repeatable as possible. The voting procedure has become very well structured, with every jury member having one vote. After each product presentation and a short private discussion by the jury, the product is immediately voted on in three rounds. In the first round, basic properties such as safety and ease of use are evaluated on a scale of one to six. Only products that reach a certain threshold move on to the next round. In the second round, they assess the product's educational value. Finally, in the third round, the jury judges the different aspects of innovation. Only products that make it into round three are eligible for an award.

While the size of the jury has been fixed, its composition has changed considerably over time. Most jury members are professors at colleges and universities from Europe, Asia, Latin America, and the United States. Their areas of expertise include education, science, sociology, educational technology, child psychology, and vocational training. Some jury members continue to serve year after year, while others drop out after participating once. In a sense, participation in the jury has been self-selecting: While the Worlddidac secretariat makes the initial selection of new jury members, reappointments are done through a mix of informal peer evaluation and evaluation by the Worlddidac secretariat. It has never been a problem to find well-qualified candidates, as the appointment carries a lot of prestige and is a great opportunity to learn about new products. Rather, the problem is to find the best suited among a large pool of potential candidates.

Peter has noticed some common traits among the most success-ful jurors during his ten-year tenure in the group. First, you need to be an expert in your field—but that's the easiest of the requirements. There are always more than enough highly competent academics and professionals interested in serving on the jury. You also have to demonstrate insatiable curiosity and the willingness to experiment and learn new things. The final criterion, though, is the hardest to meet: You need to be a fair team player.

Jurors engage in long discussions to convince their peers about the merits of this or that favorite product, and everyone has favorites. Well-performing jury members can distance themselves from their own arguments and understand the arguments of others. They have a deep sense of fairness, a willingness to collaborate, and they abstain from engaging lengthy and fruitless arguments aimed only at "win-ning." Instead, they pursue the broader goal of finding the best and most deserving products to which awards should be given. This means that they have to have a similar behavioral code, a common "genetic" mindset that makes them suitable to work together as a self-organizing swarm.

This collaboration in swarm creativity is something more. It becomes clear above and beyond the well-structured decision and coordination processes. Usually after the first day of discussing and voting on the qualities of the submitted products, Peter notices coolhunting by swarm creativity at work. The jury starts working as a single organism. It is as if each juror knows how his or her col-leagues would vote.

Whenever a vote is taken, each jury member has to press a but-ton on the voting device, submitting a value from one to six. The values pop up immediately on a large screen in front of the jury. It's impossible to tell who has voted in what way—and yet the jury "self-corrects" the overall vote, first by anticipating as a swarm how individuals are voting and then, acting as a single organism, making adjustments. For example, a music lover and hobby musician on the jury had a tendency to overrate educational music productions. The other jurors noticed this trend, and began—mostly unconsciously— to correct the skew by giving lower scores than they might otherwise have given. A mechanical engineer on the jury always favored vocational engineering training equipment with inflated grades, but other jurors made corrections—mostly unconsciously.

This may seem somehow "undemocratic" in that it seems to take away the individual's vote. But the amazing thing is that this collective decision making, this swarm creativity, is consummately democratic *and* comes up with the "right" conclusions. At the end of each year's process, the "right" selection of reviewed products gets awards. How do we know? The market and educational industry confirm the choices.

Another example of swarm creativity has to do with the ways in which the jury registers trust and both positive and negative feedback. For instance, the jury had come to trust the expert in kindergarten furniture for judgments about these submissions. Because she had shown herself to be knowledgeable, objective, and fair, the group trusted her verbal assessment of product before official voting begins—reinforcing positive feedback. Conversely, there was an expert in electrical engineering education on the jury from a country where decision making by consensus is the rule. He rarely ventured to give his personal opinion of a product. Once, when he *did* try to convince jurors of the merits of a particular product, the jury did not give too much credence to his assessment—a reinforcement of negative feedback. The kindergarten expert had built up trust by giving consistent judgment and advice on many products, while the electrical engineering expert had done very little to develop the jury's trust of his assessment capabilities, having kept himself so much in the background. When he enthusiastically recommended a single product, the jury was suspicious. The end effect was that the jury collaborated as a swarm, subconsciously compensating for each other's strengths and weaknesses.

In a nutshell, the Worlddidac awards jury offers a compelling example of discovering trends and trendsetters through swarm creativity. The winning products tend to do very well in the market, and even the presenters who don't get an award grudgingly accept the verdict. The Worlddidac award jury also illustrates the predictive capabilities of swarms, as it has been able to consistently predict future winners in the educational marketplace. In Chapter 3, we explore the predictive potential of swarms in greater depth.

3

Swarms Can Better
Predict the Future

It has always been assumed that anything as complicated as human society would quickly become chaotic and, therefore, unpredictable. What I have done, however, is to show that, in studying human society, it is possible to . . . predict the future, not in full detail, of course, but in broad sweeps.

Hari Seldon, in *Prelude to Foundation* by Isaac Asimov[1]

COOLHUNTING involves making observations and predictions as part of the search for cutting-edge trends. It is a way of capturing what the collective mind is thinking, and using what is captured to advantage. The collective mind is a powerful force and tapping into the collective mind can offer tremendous benefits. On the television series *Who Wants to Be a Millionaire?* contestants unsure of the answer to a question had the option of asking the audience or phoning a so-called expert. Far more often than did the experts, the collective intelligence of the audience produced the correct answer. This is a simple example of coolhunting through swarm creativity.

A group of people is better at solving a complex task than an expert. For example, in 1906 statistician Francis Galton came across a weight-guessing contest. An ox was on display. Everybody could submit a guess as to the weight of the ox, once it was slaughtered and dressed. To the big surprise of Galton, the average weight from the guesses of those in the crowd was almost exactly correct, while none of the so-called experts had come nearly as close. How cool would it be to unlock this collective intelligence to predict what is going to be cool?

Again, the bees offer us inspiration about predicting—in their case, it's the weather. Scientists have determined that honey bees will not go out looking for flowers or food if it is raining, or if the wind is blowing at a velocity greater than 34 kilometers per hour.[2] In fact, there's an old saying that goes like this: When bees stay close to the hive, rain is close by.

Bees are smart. In the rain, their body weight increases and makes it difficult—and sometimes impossible—to fly. In the high winds, the bees find it impossible to maneuver, and they can't get back to the hive.

If you watch the bee swarm, you can make predictions. Bee-keepers will tell you that even if there's not a cloud in the sky, when your bees are staying in the hive, or very close by, you can expect inclement weather. And even if the skies are overcast, and rain seems to threaten, bees flying excitedly out of the hive is a sign that the weather soon will change for the better.

Coolhunters can learn a lot from how the swarm behaves.

Prediction Markets

Prediction markets are one way of making use of collective intelligence to predict what is going to happen. Participants in prediction markets buy and sell assets, the financial cash value of which are tied to a particular event—for example, a U.S. presidential election. The traded assets can also be tied to a parameter such as expected sales income for the next quarter, or amount of days that a project might be late. The current market prices can then be interpreted as predictions of the probability of the event or the expected value of the parameter. In 2003, the U.S. Pentagon proposed a market in which anonymous bettors would wager on the likelihood of terrorist attacks. While the proposal was met with furious public opposition, and was quickly dropped, it confirms what we already know: prediction markets are for real.

IOWA POLITICAL MARKETS

The Iowa Electronic Markets, a group of small-scale, real-money future markets conducted by the University of Iowa College of Business, includes the Iowa Political Markets—the oldest and most famous of all predication markets. They are operated for research and teaching purposes. The idea behind these markets is to predict election outcomes, and the contracts in the markets are designed to do so.

"Predict elections via some kind of futures trading?" you say. "That doesn't seem very democratic!" The good news is that the traders are not deciding elections, only demonstrating the power of swarm creativity in figuring out who will win. The rate of accuracy is quite a bit higher than are polls. Even the question asked in the market is different than what pollsters ask, and the construction of the question celebrates the concept of swarming. Polls typically ask: If the election were being held today, do you think you would vote for Candidate X or Candidate Y? In the Iowa Markets, traders receive a financial award that is linked to answering a different question correctly: for whom will everyone vote on Election Day?

Why does the swarm creativity "work" in the Iowa Elections Market? University of Iowa researchers explain that to work in theory, the markets must have two features. One is that "there must be enough traders so that the aggregate of their knowledge can forecast correctly the outcome of the election." The second is that "the market mechanism must facilitate aggregation" of the disparate information these traders possess "so that the prevailing market price becomes a sufficient statistic for their collective information."[3] In other words, the market must be set up precisely so that the creative thinking—in this case, predicting—of the swarm as a whole can be accessible to the members of the swarm as individual traders.

Another element of what makes prediction markets work—and what helps make coolhunting and coolfarming successful—is to have "skin in the game." The Iowa market is an incentive mechanism. You put real money in, and you earn a real monetary reward if you make better forecasts and more profitable trades.

HEWLETT-PACKARD

Prediction markets are not restricted to politics. When Hewlett-Packard researcher Kay-Yeet Chen asked *all* the members of one Hewlett-Packard sales department about expected sales revenue, and not just the boss, their predictions were unusually accurate. Why? They used a market-based approach to predict how much money Hewlett-Packard would make from its products in the coming months.

Participants in the Hewlett-Packard market were staff members of the units responsible for selling the products. There were also a few HP Lab researchers, who had no first-hand knowledge about the product and sales process, but who complemented the population of traders as informed outsiders, making up their decisions based on discussions with insiders. Members of the prediction market bought and sold shares that paid off when sales fell within a certain range. Traders bought shares making predictions on the dollar amount of next month's sales, on the number of units sold next month, and on the number of units per month for the next quarter. A typical security would pay out $1 if, and only if, future sales were, say, between 1,000 and 1,500 units. Another might pay off if sales fell between 1,500 and 20,000 units. There were ten types of securities trade on the market—a range broad enough to include all the relevant possible sales outcomes. By examining the prices of all ten shares, Hewlett-Packard could assign a probability to any combination of outcomes—a more nuanced analysis than that available from a questionnaire. The company could, for example, determine the probability of sales falling anywhere below 1,000 units or anywhere above 3,000 units.

It is important that the people involved in making predictions in this way have real skin in the game, or else there is little incentive to think fully and carefully. In a COIN, this "skin in the game" is the deep commitment of its members to the overarching goal and vision of the COIN. In prediction markets, participants usually take a direct monetary interest. At Hewlett-Packard, the company subsidized participation in the information market, so that traders could not lose money. But they could keep their winnings if their predictions were accurate. This was a substantial enough incentive for participants to trade thoughtfully and carefully.

When Hewlett-Packard compared the implicit forecasts made by the prediction market with the company's own official forecasts and with actual sales figures, it found that the mean market-based prediction was significantly closer, in 15 of 16 trials, to the actual sales figure than was the official forecast. In the one remaining trial, the mean market prediction and the official forecast were equally close.

Another advantage of using prediction markets for sales forecasts is that these markets encourage traders to put their money on what they really believe, not what they may have told their bosses. A company's sales team members rarely have an incentive to tell the boss that next quarter's sales are going to be lower than expected. But by voting with their purses, sales team members have incentives to tell the truth and forecast sales as accurately as possible.

While none of the prediction market traders have perfect knowledge of all potential sales, the combined knowledge of the swarm is much more precise than is the singular knowledge of any key account manager or senior sales executive, who might be blinded by wishful thinking. And whereas sales team members might once have been motivated to pretty up the numbers because their sales forecasts influenced their compensation, their main incentive now is to predict reality as accurately as possible. Encouraged by the success of its experiment, Hewlett-Packard is now using prediction markets as a sales forecasting tool for other business divisions.

SIEMENS

Prediction markets can also be used to predict project outcomes. German engineering giant Siemens has successfully used prediction markets to forecast whether a software project would be completed on time. Modeled after the Iowa political stock market, 200 members of a large software project from Siemens Austria were given the opportunity to buy *yes* and *no* shares representing their bet on whether their project would reach milestones on time. Traders in this prediction market could also buy options on a possible delay or on being early. Participants had to invest their own money, but Siemens management tripled each trader's initial investment as a way to increase participation.

The Siemens market became much better at predicting project delays than were the project managers, and they often correctly predicted longer delays than the official forecast. It even got to the point where management started to use unexpected drops in the price of yes shares as early warning signs indicating an expected delay in reaching the next milestone. In one Siemens project, the prediction market successively decreased the value of *yes* shares until they reached junk status. Peaks in trading activity also reflected the occurrence of unexpected external events. Thus, the prediction market doubled as an indicator of events in the real world.

It's tough to be the bearer of bad news, which explains why project managers frequently are the last ones to learn about adverse developments and impending roadblocks in a project. Prediction markets offer a powerful way to circumvent this problem. Project members who are reluctant to use official communication channels to voice concerns about not reaching official deadlines will vote with their pocketbooks.

Although the Siemens prediction market was quite small—of 200 project members, only 60 decided to buy shares—it did a superb job of predicting the project's future. The share price fluctuated in the first month of a four-month project phase, but then remained stable for the remaining months, predicting a delay of two to three weeks. In other words, after the first month, market participants *other* than project management were able to predict correctly the delay.

The Siemens experiment is an application of collective intelligence. Market participants contribute their locally superior knowledge of project progress and looming obstacles to solving the problem of correctly predicting the project completion date. It does not matter that each member of the swarm has only a small subset of the full project information, because the swarm combines the pieces of the puzzle to make its predictions. As it turns out, this locally optimized aggregation of swarm knowledge is better than the global knowledge of the project leader.

HOLLYWOOD STOCK EXCHANGE

The Hollywood Stock Exchange (HSX) is another example of a prediction market that uses swarm creativity to uncover trends. Some 1.4 million registered users trade—for fun and to uncover real useful business information—on the success of movies and actors. Users are given $2 million in mock money when they register and can buy and sell movie stocks on the HSX website as soon as a film deal is announced. Two former investment bankers founded the exchange in 1996 and eventually sold it to investment bank Cantor Fitzgerald, which specializes in bond trading. Cantor makes its money on the exchange by selling online advertising and—most important—supplying data to movie studios. The studios pay for data based on HSX players' trades, and no doubt use the information to juggle investments in future films.

How accurate is this prediction market? The last of the "Star Wars" movies—*Episode III: Revenge of the Sith*—opened in May 2005 with a box-office take of $108.4 million. HSX predicted $104.8 million.

RITE-SOLUTIONS' MUTUAL FUN

The Hollywood Stock Exchange is open to anyone who wants to play. One of the best applications of an *internal* market of ideas and predictions we've seen is at Rite-Solutions, a software company with offices on the East and West coasts that, according to CEO James R. Lavoie, has "created a marketplace to harvest collective genius."[4] The company calls its internal mock stock market "Mutual Fun."

Employees are given $10,000 in pretend money to invest in ideas floated on one of the Mutual Fun's three indices: the Spazdaq for emerging technologies the company might acquire; the Bow Jones for extensions of products and services that might be considered (and which may use the Spazdaq technologies); and Savings Bonds, for cost-savings and efficiency measures to consider for implementation. Any Rite-Solution employee can propose a stock for the Mutual Fun market, and then other employees buy or sell the stocks. Stock prices are tied to the market activity, which represent what the company's computer scientists, engineers, project managers, marketers, accountants, administrative assistants—everyone who wants to "play" (as Lavoie calls it)—think of the idea.

Employees who launch a stock create an "expect-us" (like a prospectus) that explains what Rite-Solutions can do with the idea, and other employees review these documents to make their investment decisions. A ticker scrolls across Rite-Solution computer screens with stock news and updated stock prices in real time.

The premise for the Mutual Fun market is Rite-Solution's desire to "harvest" ideas actively and accrue the best results by giving everyone in the company a voice. "If you can establish a community of mutual respect and give people an outlet for their creative genius, you can have fun harvesting it," explains Lavoie.[5] To amplify the potential for swarm creativity, Mutual Fun uses "smart routing agents and threaded discussions to promote dialog between interested [employee] investors across the different offices of the company . . ."[6] Senior management gauges what direction Rite-Solution ought to go in from this collective intelligence.

Mutual Fun is one part of what appears to be a very COIN-oriented approach at Rite-Solutions. The company's vision statement on its website even uses the language of COINs, referring to "an innovative organizational concept that is more community based, relying on mutual trust, respect, and peer collaboration, rather than the authoritative structure of the hierarchy."[7] And the evidence that senior management gives power away in this way is strong.

One of the first Mutual Fun stocks was an idea for applying "three-dimensional visualization technology. . . to help sailors and domestic-security personnel practice making decisions in emergency situations."[8] The company president originally didn't like this video game-related idea, but Rite-Solution's employees overwhelmingly supported the idea with their Mutual Fun activity. The ticker symbol for the stock was VIEW, and today the Rite-View product accounts for nearly one-third of the company's total sales.

This approach to business, incorporating some of the best principles of swarm creativity and collaborative innovation, would be remarkable enough without the knowledge that the company's primary business arena is the military, and as a defense contractor specializes in creating advanced command-and-control systems for the U.S. Navy. Certainly not a customer you would normally expect to give its support to this approach to harvesting new ideas.

Birds of a Feather Flock Together: Predicting Success Based on Peer Networks

Most readers probably have a sense for the conventional wisdom that says it pays to team with competitors and form strategic alliances. It turns out that it also pays if you do no more than talk to your competitors. Our research has produced solid, scientific evidence that swarm creativity among competitors affords an advantage to collaborating firms.

Studying the communication network of 100 Israeli software companies beginning in 1998 led to the discovery that those that would fail within five years and those that would succeed within the same period were already grouping with their peers. It turns out that those who failed talked less than those that succeeded, and to the degree that they talked at all, it was to their future peers in failure.

As part of an MIT research project, we analyzed 100 software startups in Israel. The basic analysis had been done in 1999 by one of our colleagues, Ornit Raz, as part of her graduate work at Technion, one of Israel's leading universities.[9] She was looking at where the companies were located, what strategies they were pursuing, and their policies on alliances. She also asked top executives about their communication networks.

Specifically, Ornit asked the executives whether they were communicating with other executives in the 100 startups, who they were, and whether theirs was a close relationship or just an informal connection. Some 71 of the 100 companies responded to the questionnaire; of the 29 that did not respond, 24 were never mentioned by any of those who did reply to the survey. The senior management of those firms was completely isolated from their peer network of software startup executives in Israel.

Five years later, we checked back on all 100 companies to see which of them were still around and found that 42 had gone out of business. Some of the most interesting—and most surprising—data had to do with the firms that had not responded to Ornit's survey. Of the 24 isolated firms, 15 had failed. That's a pretty high percentage, given that more than half of the original group of firms had survived. While the difference might not seem big, statistically it's huge (and it's the kind of advance knowledge that could enrich investors). So, we drew our first conclusion: a willingness to reach out, communicate, and share information with others—in this instance, with Ornit—has a payback. To put it most provocatively: the simple willingness of some executives to answer the questionnaire led to a higher survival rate for their companies.

We can, of course, put this finding in a less self-referential context. Those executives willing to do something for the "common good" by taking time out of their busy schedules to answer a research questionnaire were the ones leading the companies that were still around five years after the survey was administered. This says something about the personalities of these executives, but it also suggests that investing time into public welfare and basis research, in the end, does good for the company.

We didn't stop at this finding, though. The next step of our research was to analyze the interactions. We went back to the original 100 from 1999 and analyzed the 76 firms that were "non-isolated"—in other words, that were mentioned by at least one other company. We plotted the communication network, combining all types of interactions—from ad hoc exchanges of information to strategic alliances—into one picture. Figure 3–1 illustrates what the network looked like.

The first thing to notice is that the survivors (represented by the dark dots—the nonsurvivors are the gray dots) occupy the most central positions in the network. Remember, this is the picture from 1999, before anyone had gone out of business. The future high-performing companies—that is, the companies that we would later find to be still around in 2004—are mostly located in the center of the

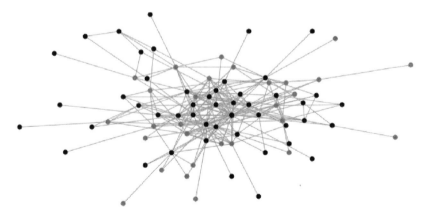

FIGURE 3–1. The communication network of Israeli software firms.

1999 communication network. More than that, though, the picture shows that high performers share their connections with their friends. Don't be a star, be a galaxy.

A central star network is precisely that—the star company in the center controls all communication, and the outlying satellite companies communicate with each other only through the intermediation of the star. It turns out, however, that the companies in the center don't need the star as an intermediary. In the communication network we were able to draw, the companies in the center are all communicating with each other directly.

When we put the Israel research project in context, this simple finding takes on a lot more significance. In 1999, when the original research was done, the e-Business craze was unfolding at a dizzying rate. Startups were popping up everywhere. Numbers of Internet users and browser clicks drove company valuations. In retrospect, few would disagree that this was a time when solid economic principles had been largely flushed down the toilet and investors seemed to have collectively lost their minds. Not long after Ornit completed her data collection for the study, the e-Business bubble burst and startup companies were going bust in droves. The interesting question for our research was this: why, in such a volatile environment, would 58 of the 100 startups survive?

Here's what we figured out. Companies that could rely on a strong network were much better able to survive the burst of the e-business bubble. As Internet startups perished across the globe, almost all of the central hubs in our 1999 peer network were still alive in 2004. They had already entered into more or less formal relationships by 1999, and partnering with their competitors helped these companies weather the storm by bundling relative strengths and relying on collaboration with peers to compensate for their weaknesses.

AnnaLee Saxenian, dean and professor in the University of California at Berkeley School of Information Management and Systems (SIMS), found something similar. She compared the mode of operations of firms in the greater Boston area with Silicon Valley companies, which had grown much more rapidly. Why? She concluded that the Silicon Valley firms benefited from their more open communication structure and their willingness to partner with competitors.[10] But her insights were based only on empirical evidence; unlike Ornit, she had no detailed records of the communication network of the executives of firms in Massachusetts and Northern California she surveyed. Our study of the 100 Israel software startups finally puts Saxenian's empirical results on a solid theoretical foundation. The picture says it loud and clear: companies—even star companies—embedded in a galaxy of communication networks with competitors have a huge competitive advantage.

Professor Saxenian looked at two distinct geographic regions, so we thought it would be a good idea to investigate whether a firm's location mattered for survival. Specifically, we wondered whether companies co-located in the Haifa region—the "Silicon Valley of Israel"—enjoyed an above-average survival rate. Somewhat to our surprise, we found that location did not matter. While executives of companies that were geographically close communicated more with each other, we could find no significant link between a firm's location near Haifa and its likelihood of surviving. Our conclusion: Companies have a fair chance of success even if they are not located within Israel's economic center. What matters much more is that the company executives talk with each other, be it face to face, over the phone, or via e-mail.

The picture becomes even more striking if we look at the self-reported close alliances among the firms (see Figure 3–2).

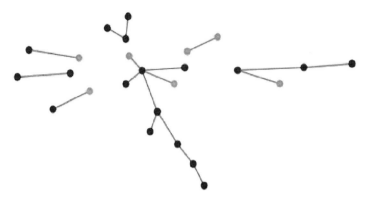

FIGURE 3–2. *Close alliances among Israeli software firms.*

Our finding in a nutshell: Almost all companies that were central communicators and embedded in strong alliances in 1999 are flourishing in 2004—despite the collapse of a huge segment of their industry. They demonstrated what we said in Chapter 2: that it's cool to share knowledge—*even with your competitors.* And now we know how to coolhunt for companies most likely to succeed, using swarm creativity. In Chapter 4, we apply what we've just learned about the power of galaxies to teams of software developers, and others.

How cool would it be if you could actually *predict* your future network?

You Can Predict Your Future Network

Predicting your future network has obvious benefits, because knowing who will play what role in a given network can really help you move a trend forward. It turns out that some aspects of network prediction are relatively straightforward. For instance, consider people who have few friends. There is a high probability that friends of people who themselves have few friends will, in the future, develop mutual friendships among themselves. Or, as Scott's high-school-age daughter puts it, "Yeah, the loners tend to hang together."

Extending this to large networks helps predict future gatekeepers and influencers. From there, you may even be able to predict which new idea is going to make it in the market, based on knowledge not only of the quality of the idea but also of the quality of the individuals and the team—the network—that supports the innovation.

David Liben-Nowell of MIT and Jon Kleinberg of Cornell University have done some valuable work on predicting networks, motivated by their interest in understanding the mechanisms by which social networks evolve. They looked at the *link prediction problem*, asking this question: "Given a snapshot of a social network, can we infer which new interactions among its members are likely to occur in the near future?"[11] They set up an experiment to determine whether it is possible to predict the edges that will be added to the network over a particular interval of time. In social network analysis, the edges characterize the social interactions between individuals or organizations.

The Liben-Nowell and Kleinberg experiment considered a coauthorship network among scientists, and suggested reasons that could develop outside of the network for two scientists who had never written a paper together actually doing so at some point in the not-too-distant future—for example, eventually finding themselves at the same institution. "Such collaborations can be hard to predict," they write.

What matters for coolhunting and predicting your future network is their sense that "a large number of new collaborations are hinted at by the topology of the network: two scientists who are 'close' in the network will have colleagues in common, and will travel in similar circles; this suggests that they themselves are more likely to collaborate in the near future." In their experiment, Liben-Nowell and Kleinberg loaded three years of coauthorship relationships data into their system. They then let their system make predictions about which authors who did not yet collaborate might be working together in the future, and checked those predictions against the subsequent three years of co-citations in the database. These researchers were able to show that, in fact, information about future interactions *can* be extracted from the structure of the network.

Future interactions are future relationships and hence future edges. Liben-Nowell and Kleinberg tried different approaches of calculating future edges, and found that birds of a feather really *do* flock together. The more similarities two people have, the higher are the chances that they will become collaborators in the future. Having common friends is a good start. Being part of the same community is better. But being someone with few friends, and sharing some of those friends with others who also have few friends, is the best predictor Liben-Nowell and Kleinberg found for future collaboration. We know this from the formulas used in their research, which show in the context of the study of coauthorship among scientists that certain predictors devised by others work best. Specifically, Liben-Nowell and Kleinberg use a formula of Lada Adamic and Eytan Adar that looks at common neighbors and weights "rarer" neighbors (people who are less linked) higher.[12] They also use a very old predictor from Leo Katz that shows that people who have common paths—that is, are in the same subcommunity—will work together.[13] This confirms the claim we made earlier: You can predict who might be in your future network.

As Adamic and Adar write, "Knowing which friend of a friend is involved in a particular activity can help users find a chain of acquaintances to reach the people they need to." The networks they found online "open a whole range of possibilities in marketing research, from identifying which groups might be interested in a product to relying on the social network to propagate information about that product."

What's the value for coolhunting? Predicting future connections will permit you to do "what-if" simulations that, in turn, predict who might become a trendsetter. How cool will it be to know not only who is a trendsetter today, but also who might become a trendsetter tomorrow?

4

About Trendsetters

I therefore put myself as much as I could out of sight, and stated it as a scheme of a num-
ber of friends, who had requested me to go about and propose it to such as they thought
lovers of reading. In this way my affair went on more smoothly, and I ever after prac-
tis'd it on such occasions; and, from my frequent successes, can heartily recommend it.
The present little sacrifice of your vanity will afterwards be amply repaid.

—Benjamin Franklin[1]

COOL PEOPLE disseminate cool trends. In this chapter, we look at
the people who are the carriers of innovation. The first among these
people are, of course, the inventors. For the purposes of coolhunting, however, the early adopters and improvers of new ideas are even
more important. They are the people who convince others that the
time has come to adopt an innovation.

History gives us some great examples. Some of them are not
nearly as well known as they ought to be, given just how crucial
to the development of our modern world the efforts of these

trendsetters really were. Consider one from the middle of the seventeenth century.

Before 1660, in the midst of a fervent of scientific discovery throughout Europe, findings were shared only by individuals corresponding with each other. That all changed when a group of scientists and intellectuals in England formed the Royal Society of London for Improving Natural Knowledge—commonly known as the Royal Society. The objective was greater diffusion of information.

One of the founders was Henry Oldenburg—an avid correspondent. He became the Royal Society's secretary and established a systematic organization of correspondence for the diffusion of information. Oldenburg was particularly well suited to the task, as he was considered to be a "methodical, conscientious, hard-working individual."[2] He managed to attract others to the task throughout Europe, even in the continent's farthest reaches, and it wasn't long before there was a complex network by which scientific information was exchanged.

Oldenburg worked hard to keep the momentum that would eventually become the model for scientific organizations the world over. He would regularly report to Society meetings on newly gained knowledge. With a messianic zeal, he wrote to leading scientists in other countries to urge their participation in the growing knowledge network. In a January 1662 letter to Johannes Hevelius, a Polish astronomer today known as the "founder of lunar topography," he urged him to engage with the Royal Society in sharing knowledge:

> It is now our business . . . to attract to the same purpose men from all parts of the world who are famous for their learning to exhort [them] to unwearied efforts. Indeed, friendship among learned men is a great aid to the investigation and

elucidation of truth; if some friendship could be spread among those whose minds are unfettered and above partisan zeal . . . philosophy would be raised to its greatest heights.[3]

Oldenburg asked Hevelius to report regularly to the Society on his work, and promised that in return he would keep Hevelius informed of whatever new astronomical knowledge came through the Society's network. Hevelius seemed only too happy to comply.

A few years later, Oldenburg launched what is today the world's oldest continuously published scientific journal, *Philosophical Transactions*. It was his idea for another way to diffuse information.

Through his work with the Royal Society over a seventeen-year period, Oldenburg—and the Collaborative Innovation Network he had nurtured—played a central role in getting the work of one thinker into the hands of one of the world's most important scientists, and then the latter's work out to a wider audience. In 1670, a young mathematician and philosopher named Gottfried Wilhelm von Leibniz sent a letter to Oldenburg from his home in Leipzig, Germany. "Pardon the fact that I, an unknown person, write to one who is not unknown; for to what man who has heard of the Royal Society can you be unknown?" wrote Leibniz. "And who has not heard of the Society, if he is in any way drawn to an interest in true learning?"

Leibniz was studying motion, and shared his theories with Oldenburg—who in turn connected what Leibniz was doing with the similar work being undertaken by other German scientists. Leibniz and Oldenburg continued to correspond, and in 1673 the Royal Society named Leibniz a Fellow. He continued his wide-ranging work, and the next year informed Oldenburg of his work on infinitesimals in mathematics.[4] Oldenburg, in turn, shared with Leibniz that Isaac Newton had found some general methods related to infinitesimals. Oldenburg was, in fact, the first to communicate about Newton's mathematical work beyond England.

Eventually, both working on calculus, Leibniz and Newton would correspond directly. And while history shows that there was a significant intellectual dispute between the two over their respective approaches to this mathematical conundrum, there is no doubt that without the work of Henry Oldenburg and his vision of sharing information for the greater good, the great advances of the seventeenth century might not have come until much later.

Oldenburg saw himself as part of a larger galaxy of scientists and philosophers, each with something to offer the others. He is a shining example, but one we like even more is that of Benjamin Franklin, an archetypical leader of a Collaborative Innovation Network. Franklin illustrates many of the traits of a great COIN leader. Understand Ben's characteristics, and you're better armed to look for other trendsetters.

Benjamin Franklin as Role Model

Benjamin Franklin sets a great example and role model as a lifelong trendsetter and innovator. His list of inventions is legend: the lightning rod, bifocals, the odometer, the Franklin stove. But perhaps most impressive is that he gave away his innovations for free. Franklin voluntarily relinquished all patent rights to his inventions.

Franklin was an outgoing, intelligent individual who loved to sit down and have long conversations with friends and acquaintances. To give some structure to his passion for discussion, he established a club dedicated to "mutual improvement." The year was 1727, and Franklin was twenty-one years old.

Franklin called his club the Junto—Latin for "meeting"—and invited people from his wide circle of friends in Philadelphia to join. They included people with diverse backgrounds and from varying occupations, but what they shared with Franklin was a spirit of inquiry, a strong desire for self-improvement, a commitment to helping others, and a real sense of community. Like Franklin, they were also men who possessed a sizable collection of books. In fact, Franklin had met many of them in his quest for books to borrow in those days before public libraries.

At the Junto, which functioned as a private forum, members debated questions of morals, politics, natural philosophy, and physics. They exchanged knowledge about business affairs. To ensure that the gatherings were productive and that valuable conversation would ensue, there was a formal structure to Junto meetings. It was Franklin's plan, and it was also meant to promote self-education. Each member was expected to come prepared to share an essay he had written on some important topic, such as a pressing issue of the day, or a question in philosophy, or that reflected on community happenings, or that recounted experiences with important or fascinating people.

In Junto discussions members often referred to books with which other members might not have been familiar. Franklin hit upon the idea that members should pool their book collections and store them at the Junto's meeting place. "By thus clubbing our books to a common library," wrote Franklin in his *Autobiography*, "we should, while we lik'd to keep them together, have each of us the advantage of using the books of all the other members, which would be nearly as beneficial as if each owned the whole." After a year of suffering under insufficient care, the books were returned to their owners—but the experiment gave Franklin an idea. On July 1, 1731, Franklin proposed what later became the Library Company of Philadelphia. This was the first subscription library, and it became a model for numerous similar libraries throughout the American colonies.

Libraries available for public use were but one idea that grew out of the Junto discussions. Another was that for volunteer fire departments. During a visit to his hometown of Boston, Franklin noticed that the city seemed considerably more prepared than was Philadelphia to fight fires. Returning to Pennsylvania, he consulted the Junto for ideas on how better to combat fires. Swarm creativity ruled the day, and the ideas generated were published in articles and letters between 1733 and 1736 in the *Pennsylvania Gazette*, which engaged the public in the discussion. In the articles, Franklin pointed to the inadequacy of Philadelphia fire-fighting and suggested things citizens could do, "according to their abilities," to help.

Franklin's persistence paid off. In December 1736, a group of thirty Philadelphia men formed the Union Fire Company. They met monthly to discuss fire prevention and fire-fighting methods, and adopted among their equipment "leather buckets with strong bags and baskets (for packing and transporting goods)"—which were brought to every fire and soon became a regular fixture in Philadelphia homes.

Franklin's Junto—an early and archetypal Collaborative Innovation Network—lasted for forty years. It reflected Franklin's conviction that learning only from oneself is foolish and that a good social network is essential to self-education. More than that, Franklin employed the Junto COIN as the main means to disseminate his innovations and create new trends. Its members were instrumental as ardent supporters, early adopters, and constructive critics of Franklin's ideas.

Benjamin Franklin brought together like-minded individuals in his COIN, but he always functioned as a galaxy. He gained power by giving it away, generously and freely shared knowledge, and trusted self-organization and swarm creativity. Like a worker bee in a beehive, and like Henry Oldenburg before him, Franklin knew that advancing knowledge and innovation was best served if he stepped out of the limelight. His is a valuable lesson for and example of coolhunting.

We find an excellent *negative* example in the history of hypertext.

The Anti-Ben?

In July 1945, Dr. Vannevar Bush—then the science advisor to President Franklin Roosevelt—proposed the idea of "Memex" in a now-famous article in *The Atlantic Monthly*, "As We May Think." Bush set out the idea for a machine that would store both text and graphics and with which it would be possible to link any one piece of information to another. The user of Memex would be able to create an information trail of traveled links, and the trail could be stored and retrieved later. Even though Bush conceived of Memex on microfilm, his idea became the basis for today's World Wide Web.

Some twenty years later, in 1965, Ted Nelson—a self-styled philosopher—delivered a paper to the national conference of the Association for Computing Machinery, in which he coined the term "hypertext." He influenced several developers of the Internet. Subsequently, Dr. Andries van Dam, at Brown University in Providence, Rhode Island, led a team to develop the first hypertext-based system. Others followed, and eventually, in 1991—we're truncating the story here quite a bit—Tim Berners-Lee released the World Wide Web.

Along the way, Ted Nelson popularized the hypertext concept in his book *Literary Machines*, and expounded his vision of a universe of documents, which he called a "docuverse," where all data were stored once and forever, and where all information would be accessible to anyone via a link from anywhere else. The World Wide Web, although there are deletions and some information is stored in multiple locations, is a close approximation of Nelson's idea.

Ted Nelson is most definitely an innovator, but he is certainly no trendsetter. By our definition, what distinguishes a "mere" innovator from a genuine trendsetter is that the trendsetter behaves not like a star, but as a galaxy, giving away power and building collaborative creativity. It's no accident that Tim Berners-Lee is pretty well known even among people who aren't technology geeks, but Ted Nelson remained virtually anonymous to the same group.

So, where is the negative example promised above? Ted Nelson, a visionary whose ideas touched one of the most important trendsetters of our time, tells us in his own words about how *not* to build collaborative innovation. In 1996, he was interviewed on "The Cyberspace Report," a public affairs radio show that aired on KUCI in Irvine, California.[5] The interviewer was Jim Whitehead, who asked Nelson how, based on his own experience, he would encourage people with visionary ideas to go about turning them into reality.

Here's Nelson's answer: "What would I recommend to a young visionary today? Very straightforward, learn to deal with short-term goals and not delegate. I trusted them—famous last words." Among the "them" to whom Nelson refers is Tim Berners-Lee—who, as we show in Chapter 5, clearly knew how to be a galaxy.

Bees, too, know how to be galaxies and work cooperatively. They continue to offer us lessons. Consider, for example, those bees who have the job of scout. Whenever a scout bee discovers a rich, new food source—that's the scout's job—the scout returns to the hive and recruits other bees to her discovery. The objective is always the same: keep the swarm enjoying the richest available patches of pollen and everything else the bees like.

How does the scout bee do her recruiting? It all depends on where the food source is, but in either case it involves dancing. Karl von Frisch (1886-1982), an Austrian zoologist and winner of the 1973

Nobel Prize in Medicine and Physiology, first identified the "round dance," performed for food sources 50 to 80 meters away from the hive, and the "waggle dance" for distant floral sites. In the round dance, the scout bee convinces others in the hive to fly out and search, using olfactory and visual cues, for flowers close by, but not in any specific direction. For the waggle dance, the scout bee comes home with some nectar, crawls into the vertical combs near the hive entrance, and dances for several minutes. Frisch revealed, and later scientists confirmed, that the direction and duration of parts of the waggle dance are actually correlated with the direction and distance of the flower patch the scout bee is advocating.[6] What's notable is what never happens. Never does the scout bee return to the hive, choose a few other bees to tell about her discovery, and then set out to make a new swarm using the new food source. Everything the scout bee finds is shared with the entire hive. She knows that getting the entire hive behind her discovery is the best way to win. When the entire hive is strengthened and nurtured, so is she.

The scout bee may come back to the hive a star—after all, she's made quite an important discovery—but her behavior is nothing but that of a galaxy.

Don't Be a Star, Be a Galaxy

A gentleman we know who is active in bringing together entrepreneurs and innovators—we'll call him Fred—learned about Collaborative Innovation Networks and was inspired to create an innovation community. He selected a general topic he thought would be interesting, engaging, and would lend itself to discussion and further development. Then he identified forty people he knew—all "smart thinkers," as he called them—to get together and brainstorm about the topic. He lured the invitees to this lunch meeting in part by choosing a nice place and arranging for some good food to be served. Then he invited us to the birth of his Collaborative Innovation Network.

Fred had told the forty invitees what the general topic was so they could begin to think about it. After everyone had arrived, he began the meeting and asked each person to introduce himself or herself and give a couple of minutes' overview of their thinking. After everyone had finished, Fred announced that it was time to start talking to each other.

His dream was that a community—a COIN—would emerge from this initial meeting. But while some of the conversation was pleasant enough, very little of substance unfolded. Fred's COIN was stillborn.

Why did this happen? Why couldn't a group of forty smart people, given a worthy topic to consider—a topic that held out considerable promise as a sphere for genuine innovation—create the collaborative community Fred was anticipating? The answer is simple: Fred was a *star*. And the only thing connecting those forty people together was that they all knew Fred and that he knew them. They orbited Fred the Star. The meeting—indeed, the very way in which Fred set up the meeting—offered no opportunity for those who attended to develop commitment to the idea of collaboration. With Fred at the center, there was no way those people could form a rich network. They had a star attracting them, but they needed to be a galaxy.

Let's make this somewhat abstract principle—*don't be a star, be a galaxy*—more concrete. What did Fred do wrong? What was missing?

First, the very way in which the group was brought together was highly artificial. There was only one common denominator among all those people. Every woman and man in the room knew Fred. And there certainly wasn't any real *commitment* to a common purpose involved in attending the meeting, unless you count the willingness to sit together for a few hours in a nice room, meet some other "interesting" people, and eat good food. Fred's meeting was more a party than the birth of a collaborative innovation network, formed around a shared goal and interest.

Although Fred deserves credit for the initiative he took in trying to start a community of interest around an innovation topic, just imagine the possibilities if Fred had done a few things differently. For one, what if there had been a mechanism by which those invited had been able to discern whether the meeting was worth attending (something more substantive than the lure of good food)? In fact, what if there had been no meeting set up, but rather that the possibility of a future meeting had been left to a process of self-selection?

The group was never given an opportunity to build some genuine commitment in advance of any meeting—an absolute neonatal necessity for a successful collaborative community. Fred the Star decided who belonged, based on his personal vision of what should unfold. The participants themselves, though, brought together on this very general premise, had no basis upon which to self-select with respect to their expertise in or knowledge of the topic, level of interest, or sense of whether their participation was appropriate.

The most serious shortcoming at Fred's meeting was that there was no obstacle to overcome to join the group, unless you count the awful traffic that day. An obstacle is a critical component of self-selection. Absent any obstacles, the lure of good food is a pretty powerful one, and the important elements of self-selection are easy to ignore.

While Fred tried to be a bee, his waggle dance was awfully weak. He tried to convince the others to share what they knew, but the incentive to convert Fred's effort into a persistent community was just not there. One of his main problems was that while he did his waggle dance very actively, he had no pollen to offer. There was no common intrinsic motivation for Fred's swarm to collaborate. The swarm, therefore, refused to take Fred's lead and follow him to new pastures in creating a new COIN. It never took off.

Now imagine Fred doing things differently. First, he sends an e-mail to all 40 people, with the list visible to everyone. He outlines the general topic he thinks would be interesting to discuss, and asks those who might be interested whether they have a point of view. He offers as an incentive to those who may be interested that he'll send a follow-up message that distills the salient ideas expressed by anyone who responds. There's no mention of any meeting. Some people express a point of view, and others decline. A few others don't even answer the e-mail.

With this approach, Fred gives the e-mail recipients some indication of what to expect. He empowers them to make their own decision as to whether to participate by expressing their point of view in response to the e-mail, on the basis of some knowledge.

Now let's contrast the way in which Fred tried to create a COIN with how innovation—in this case, the creation of new consulting services—happens at Deloitte Consulting.

At Deloitte Consulting, there are plenty of stars, as you would expect. They crave the spotlight. They have big egos. They make a lot of money, and they have a lot of clients. But one thing they don't do is create successful new consulting products. They are not the source for new methods and tools that can be proposed to customers, turn into real projects, and generate new revenue.

Most successful products at Deloitte, as elsewhere, are created by the most successful team players. They collaborate in *galaxies*. Okay, you say, galaxies are made up of stars, so this is a rather false dichotomy. But in the world of coolhunting, coolfarming, swarm creativity, and collaborative innovation, the distinction between the two is decisive. The team players may be stars, but they see themselves first and foremost as part of a galaxy. They are not stars like our sun, with planets revolving around them and dependent upon them.

Don't be a star, be a galaxy. Sure, you may be a star, but if you have what seems like a great idea, why not share it with others? Why not find out who else might be interested and have something to offer to developing that idea? If there's a spotlight to be had, why not share it?

At Deloitte, galaxies work together as teams, operating not on hierarchy or on star status but on the principles of a meritocracy, where skills, knowledge, commitment, and will are rewarded. We're not talking about an egalitarian system: you do have to perform to succeed in a meritocracy, but performance is what counts, and the process is transparent.

One of the galaxies at Deloitte was started by a mid-level consultant named Tom, who had a promising idea for a new consulting product, which he floated with some friends in various offices in Europe, the United States, and Southeast Asia. Over a short time, several of them "swarmed" together around this idea. They came from all levels of the company, including a couple of partners. Hierarchical position was irrelevant. What created this swarm were the very factors missing in Fred's story. Most important was a shared purpose and goals, created over a number of weeks as the emerging collaborative innovation network shared e-mails, set up websites where they could float more ideas and discuss them, and—eventually—met face to face. The most dedicated members of the new COIN convinced their managers to pay the expense of traveling to Zurich for a working meeting where the idea would be developed into a Deloitte service offering.

After this meeting in Zurich, things became really productive. A few more weeks passed, and swarm creativity had resulted in a new consulting method, a software product, and a marketing package.

From initial idea in an e-mail sent to a number of acquaintances to selling the first engagement to a Deloitte client was a mere two months, and the product—CKN Diagnostic—was unique and very *cool.* It combined a Web-based software package that could be used to assess an organization's readiness for Collaborative Knowledge Networks with a method to improve collaborative innovation. A number of senior consulting partners embraced CKN Diagnostic as soon as it was out and helped win and deliver some major engagements for Deloitte.

Collaborative Knowledge Network

A Collaborative Knowledge Network (CKN) is an ecosystem created by three types of virtual communities:

1. *Collaborative Interest Networks,* comprising people who share the same interests but who do little actual work together in a virtual team

2. *Collaborative Learning Networks,* comprising people who come together in a community and share not only a common interest but also common knowledge and a common practice

3. *Collaborative Innovation Networks,* which are cyberteams of self-motivated people with a collective vision, enabled by the Web to collaborate in achieving a common goal by sharing ideas, information, and work

---

The CKN ecosystem is a high-speed feedback loop in which the innovative results of a COIN are immediately taken up and tested, refined, or rejected by learning and interest networks, and fed back to the originating COIN. It is the main mechanism by which to carry COIN innovations over the tipping point to adoption.

What happened at Deloitte Consulting helped give birth to the very concept of COINs. CKN Diagnostic discovered emerging collaborative innovation in the organizations where it was used. In other words, it was *coolhunting* new Collaborative Innovation Networks. Plus, the product itself had been developed by a COIN.

Unlike Fred's approach, Tom succeeded precisely by being a galaxy, not a star. He helped form an intrinsically motivated group that was interested in exploring the concept of virtual communities. This group turned this shared interest into a Deloitte service offering, but the motivation was not to garner an immediate or individual reward, but rather to develop the concept *irrespective* of any reward.

It's important not to mistake what happened as altruism. It's not that the participants had no sense for what might become of their collaboration. Each and every one knew, either intuitively or explicitly, that there *might* be some business value to participating in the collaboration network. They knew that if they succeeded, they would get the opportunity to be leaders in a cool new service area, perhaps increase their billable hours, and thus greatly improved their individual prospects for promotion and higher compensation. What more could a management consultant ask for? But it is not hyperbole to say that what mattered most to all the participants, once the self-selection process had pared the collaborative network down to its appropriate members, was that the collaboration itself was *interesting* and *engaging*. This cannot be minimized; in fact, it may well be the greatest altruism of all. In theory, a good management consultant can always find a way to extract another billable hour from a client simply by expanding the scope of typical consulting work. These folks at Deloitte were blazing a new path.

The coffee shop in Scott's Boston-area neighborhood is a good, simple example of what we mean by the galaxy idea. Independently owned, the shop is somewhat reminiscent of Starbucks, which we discuss further in Chapter 11. The attractive menu includes espresso and cappuccino as well as baked goods and a few home-made gourmet sandwiches. There are several small tables and chairs, a couch, a few overstuffed living-room type chairs, and even some toys for kids. And, notably, there is wireless access to the Internet—at no charge (a big difference from that national chain).

Peter M. (not the author of this book) is the owner. He acknowl-edges that people come in with their laptop computers, plunk down in one spot, and often stay for hours at a time. Over that period, they may purchase a couple of drinks and maybe something to eat in between. They certainly don't generate the kind of revenue per square foot that grocery stores expect, or many other retail businesses. Asked how he makes money with that kind of business model, he assures us that his customers "generate cash in the register."

What really stands out, though, is the not-so-visible network that the coffee shop has created. "People come in and work for a while, sometimes for hours at a time. They check their e-mail and perhaps talk on their mobile phones, and they tell people where they are," Peter M. says. "It's still too soon to say with definite proof, but I think this generates a lot of business for us. It creates that 'talk' about a comfortable place where you can sit and have a cup of coffee and check your e-mail." And there's no pressure to leave.

One group of coworkers uses the coffee shop on a regular basis. Their business involves a lot of visits to other stores in the west sub-urbs of Boston, and individuals in the group will come in for a quick cup of coffee, check their e-mail, and move on after only a half-hour or so. On other days, the entire group will converge at lunchtime and have a business meeting in this inviting space.

Without knowing it, Peter M. has built a small galaxy. Networking happens at his coffee shop. Business deals are made.

The authors did a lot of their brainstorming for this book in a similar place. Scott also interviewed candidates for an editorial assistant position over a two-day period at Peter M.'s coffee shop, and found the right person at one of those tables. Regulars who don't know each other get to know each other after sitting at adjacent tables for weeks at a time. Who knows? A big trend could be unleashed from a chance encounter in this small galaxy. As social network analysis research has shown, it is the "weak ties" created in places such as this coffee shop that matter most in things like helping us find new jobs and forging the links to come up with new ideas.[7]

No one tells Peter M.'s customers to hurry up and give the table to the next person. The power to determine how to behave in this small galaxy rests with the customers.

Galaxies Are High Performers

Open-source programmers are building great software at a fraction of the cost of commercial software developers. They also provide a wonderful test bed to study innovation teams working together in swarm creativity. The roles of team members are well defined, role descriptions are externally accessible, and communication archives such as online forums and mailing lists are readily available. The motivations of open-source developers also lend themselves to our inquiry: These programmers are not paid to develop their software, so money is not what drives their willingness to invest substantial time and effort into their work. Rather, they are motivated by the opportunity to collaborate with peers, to learn new skills, and by the sheer pleasure of creating new products.

One of our research projects analyzed the creativity and performance of open source developers working on Eclipse, by many criteria one of the best Java software development environments. One thing that really makes Eclipse stand apart from its commercial competitors is that it is available for free and anyone can get the source code, but that access to source code means anyone can extend and modify the software at will.

We collected the mailing lists of thirty-three Eclipse development groups. Analyzing the communication logs, we discovered who were the leaders, core contributors, and casual participants in each team. We measured how rapidly a team fixed software errors ("bugs") submitted to them by the users of their software—what we'll call the team's "performance." We also measured the "creativity" of each project team by looking at the number of enhancements and new features the developers integrated into their software product.

There were huge differences among the teams. Some fixed just a few bugs but implemented scores of new features. Others were very efficient in fixing software problems but had scant new features. We wondered whether there was a way to *predict* the performance and creativity of software teams. After an initial analysis, it turned out that the teams most efficient in fixing their bugs were simply not very good in creating new features. The opposite was also true: the most creative teams of open source developers were relatively slow in fixing their bugs. It seems all other things being equal, teams excel either in creativity or efficiency, but rarely in both. This finding, though, didn't help answer our original question: what are the characteristics of a high-performing team, what are the characteristics of a highly creative team, and is there a way to predict which will be which? We turned to their communication structures.

Our examination of the ways in which the thirty-three Eclipse teams communicated revealed two basic communication structures. Some teams had a *galaxy* structure, in which team members all spoke to each other in a democratic way. In these teams, communication intensity was quite high, with each core team member talking directly with all other core team members. By contrast, the remaining teams had a *star* structure, with one or more stars in the center who spoke to all team members, but in which the other team members had very little interaction between and among themselves. In these teams, the central stars controlled the communication flow. When we compared these two "types" of teams along the performance dimension—fixing bugs—it turned out that the galaxies were more efficient than were the stars. And when we looked at creativity, we found the same thing.

Some important variation in this finding emerged when we looked at whether the communication structures had shifted over time. High-performing teams maintain a communication structure in which the roles of central coordinator and supporting members, who are more peripheral, remain relatively constant. In highly creative teams, though, we observe a high level of creative chaos. Periods of centralized control give way to periods of total connectedness and democracy in which everyone is exchanging ideas. While the predominant communication pattern is democratic within these latter periods, there are short intersections of centralized communication where one team member dominates the discussion flow by aggressively pushing a new idea.

Studying the Eclipse developers showed that we could predict the high-performing teams, but also revealed that if we want to find trendsetters we needed to look for teams that were initially communicating in a galaxy structure. Within those galaxies, the *trendsetters* are the most connected people. They are spreading out the new ideas. They look very different from the stars, surrounded by but stifling direct action among their satellites—that is, stars who are autocratically controlling the flow of communication. Sure, those stars might lead efficient or productive teams, but new ideas are not likely to be coming out of those teams.

If you can coolhunt who will win and who will be the trendsetters, how cool would it be not only to predict your own future network but to use your coolhunting skills to establish yourself in the winning, trendsetting network?

5

Coolhunters Look for Coolfarmers

The pie keeps growing because things that look like wants today are needs tomorrow.
— Marc Andreessen, co-founder of Netscape[1]

THERE ARE, in essence, two ways to discover new trends and trend-setters. So far, we have discussed only *coolhunting*—hunting for trends by observing people through the Web, blogs, newspapers and magazines, broadcast media, and society at large to spot the new things that will become cool. Another way is *coolfarming*—getting involved in the actual creation of new trends by nurturing and cultivating new ideas.

A coolhunter observes communities and society, while a coolfarmer is personally engaged in the process of creating cool trends.

A coolfarmer does not have to be in control of the new idea to make it succeed. Rather, a coolfarmer is part of a Collaborative Innovation Network that works together in swarm creativity to bring a shared vision to reality. Think of Benjamin Franklin. As a member of the Junto, he was coolfarming many new trends.

To spot new trends, all a coolhunter has to do is look for the coolfarmers. That is precisely what Peter's friend Wayne does for a living.

Coolhunting for Trendsetters

Wayne is a professional coolhunter. As the publisher of a highly specialized series of technical books, he is always trying to spot new trends in the academic domains that correspond to his publishing activities.

"To succeed as a publisher of theoretical textbooks, you need to be slightly ahead of the adoption curve," Wayne says. "You have to be among the first to identify new trends that deserve special discussion in a book." But spotting the trends is not enough. Once Wayne has identified new trends, he also needs to find the academics willing and capable of covering those trends in writing.

Wayne's track record is impressive. Over his distinguished career at different publishing houses, he has landed many bestselling textbooks. Many books by his authors have garnered prestigious awards. How does Wayne do his coolhunting? Over lunch, Wayne explained his basic operating principles:

> I am looking for the people, not for the trends. I am trying to find the leading researchers in the field who are also 'leaders' in the other sense of the word. They are respected not only for their scientific achievements, but also because they are great mentors and role models. Of course, I go to academic

conferences in the fields where I publish. At the conferences, though, I am much more interested in the people presenting their ideas than in their basic ideas.

I try to find the trendsetters who are blazing new trails in their domains—people who are well respected by their peers for both scientific achievements and social competency. I'm not looking for the 'prima donnas' and egomaniacs, but for people who are also networkers and connectors. These trendsetters have usually dabbled in many different fields, periodically reinventing themselves. Usually, they combine a professional degree such as an MD with an academic PhD, and frequently throw in an MBA to round it all up. They are connectors—their personal network reaches into many different fields, combining academia with business, and sometimes even political contacts.

Wayne brought up the example of Robert Langer, one of the world's leading experts in tissue engineering. Langer is at the forefront of artificially recreating human organs to help sick and injured patients. He is an MIT Institute Professor, holds 800 patents, and has won many research prizes. He also runs a huge research lab and serves on numerous U.S. national academic and scientific advisory committees. Langer, highly respected in the scientific community, is considered a great mentor, and surrounds himself with bright young scientists.

In a Science magazine profile of Langer's MIT research facilities,[2] the author, Gretchen Vogel, notes that "if the chemical engineering lab were an independent company, it would dwarf many of the biotech startups in the Cambridge area." Vogel notes a big difference between those biotech firms and Langer's operation, however—none of Langer's researchers "get stock options, high salaries, or other lucrative financial inducements." His researchers are all intrinsically motivated COIN members. Their incentives are the chance to do work at the cutting edge of research in their fields and publish in the world's leading scientific journals. They earn an edge in the race to become leading academics or biotech entrepreneurs themselves. Langer's twenty post-doctoral fellows, fifteen graduate students, three or four visiting professors, and two dozen undergraduates get the chance to give talks at major meetings and be interviewed by the media.

One of Langer's lab members, researcher Prasad Shastri, spoke with reporters from *New Scientist,* the PBS program "Nova," and the Discovery Channel when his work on electrically stimulated nerve regeneration attracted attention. "Langer doesn't think the project is successful just because of him," Shastri told *Science.*

Langer's approach is to encourage lab members to take the initiative, rather than give orders. "I give people a very open environment. . . . I'm just there to act as a guide," he says. He wants his post-docs to learn how to be critical thinkers, to get them "to the point where they're asking questions rather than looking for answers." He makes time for his students and lab members to keep the collaboration going full-throttle, and every lab member has an "open invitation to schedule a meeting in his appointment book."

Langer is a galaxy, and not a star. While he is undoubtedly in the center of his galaxy, he encourages his lab members to build their own networks. Many of Langer's former students have now grown to be famous professors themselves, becoming the centers of their own galaxies. In that sense, Langer is growing an entire ecosystem of galaxies.

Wayne—our coolhunting publisher—has every reason to seek access to people like Langer. He not only learns from Langer about the latest trends in tissue engineering, but he also gains access to

Langer's network of leading researchers and up-and-coming post-docs. Wayne relies on people like Langer for his talent spotting. Langer not only tells Wayne what the trends are, but also which trendsetters Wayne should try to recruit as book authors.

Langer is an archetypical coolfarmer and trendsetter; Wayne is an archetypical coolhunter. Wayne has built his own galaxy for cool-hunting. Langer's network is firmly anchored in bioengineering; Wayne's galaxy covers a much broader domain, connecting publishers and authors from fields as diverse as mathematics, security and privacy, image processing, nanotechnology, and bioengineering. While he has a first-rate education, Wayne is not a technician by training. Nevertheless, he is unusually successful in spotting emerging trends, and in recruiting prolific writers willing to write the next textbook in cool, emerging areas. He defines coolhunting.

To gain a better understanding of coolfarming, let's look at how new ideas spread out through swarm creativity and become actual trends. The process involves three steps:

1. Invent

2. Create

3. Sell

From Idea to Trend

In the first step, *invent*, a lonely genius/inventor comes up with a new, earth-shattering idea. But lonely geniuses often have a difficult time building alliances and support for their ideas, and so the ideas remain ideas. It takes people in the second step, *create*, to take these ideas and convert them into trends.

This is where coolfarming comes in. Trendsetters work together in Collaborative Innovation Networks. Driven by deep internal

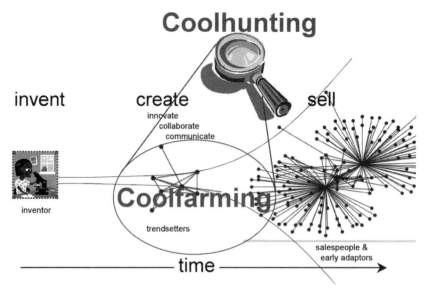

FIGURE 5–1. Creating a trend through swarm creativity

motivation and commitment, they innovate, collaborate, and communicate together and with the rest of the world to make their shared vision come true. Using their social skills, they generate enough of a stir and excitement to catch the attention of others, and soon people want to jump on the bandwagon and become part of the new trend—which the COIN established by working together in swarm creativity.

In the third step, *sell*, they recruit the people who sell the innovation to the outside world, carrying it over the tipping point. Coolfarming includes the "create" step, where the trendsetters get together to nurture and grow their vision into a real trend. It also includes the transition to the "sell" step, where the trend is adopted by the rest of the world. This adoption of the innovation in the "sell" phase follows the process defined by Everett Rogers, which we described in Chapter 1. Figure 5–1 illustrates the process. There are many commercial examples of this process.

First, though, let's explore the basic principles of coolfarming by looking at how a group of Dada artists created the multimedia CD "Enhanced Gravity."

Coolfarming "Enhanced Gravity"

While working on his previous book, *Swarm Creativity*, Peter put an early version on the Web for comment. One day, an e-mail arrived from Richard, the owner of Yucca Tree, a record label that had issued the music CD "Oppera"—the creation of which was described in the online manuscript. Richard had stumbled across the description of how swarm creativity had created "Oppera," and was really excited to read about COINs.

Richard told Peter an amazing story of how another Yucca Tree release, the multimedia CD "Enhanced Gravity," was created. The story turned out to be about coolfarming.

Richard already had a long track record of bringing "impossible" art projects to fruition. In 1983, with a friend, he launched a "Dada-zine" called NOP against the advice of all his friends, who told him it would never succeed. But Richard and his friend realized 11 issues over the course of the next years.

Richard was part of a movement called MAIL ART—a form of art-making born in the pre-punk period of the 1960s and 1970s. In many respects, MAIL ART was an early, independent, self-organized, and self-motivated art environment and art culture. All communications about and resulting in common artwork was done via postal mail (this was in the pre-Internet days). MAIL ART functions like a COIN—and without any commercial interests. The resulting artwork is mainly for the participating artists. Items created through MAIL ART are not as important as the process of working together using mail. You cannot expect to receive MAIL ART if you don't also send MAIL ART. All ideas, results, and costs are shared.

Richard used the MAIL ART process to initiate and complete music projects for his Yucca Tree label. For example, he got together a group of MAIL ARTists to create the multimedia CD "Enhanced Gravity"—a compelling example of the power of swarm creativity. Figure 5–2 shows the cover.

Over three years of hard work, the team put together an art CD that combined nine music pieces and a fully illustrated multimedia section. The music CD/CD-ROM presents a scientific, Dadaist, and humorous view of contemporary satire, and offers the user a deep view of physics, metaphysics, and visualizations of different forms of gravity.

The "Enhanced Gravity" project was organized as a COIN. No one made any money, nor are they ever likely to make any money. Richard rounded up his team by instigating a swarm, and the COIN was born through networking. Some contributors were friends of

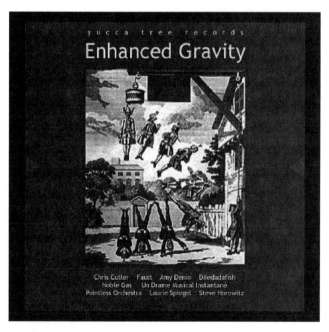

FIGURE 5–2. CD cover of Enhanced Gravity.

Richard; others had collaborated in earlier projects. One potential team member had told the group that all music CDs were being issued as multimedia "enhanced" CDs. So, the CD parodying gravity would be called "Enhanced Gravity."

The COIN members had to agree on a clear schedule for the project, as well as on definitions of the titles of pieces and the scientific, musical, and Dadaist interpretations of each title. These requirements led to serious artistic breakdowns but also acted as a motivating driver.

In the end, a rather chaotic and self-organizing multimedia project grew out of the initial idea to produce a mini-CD. Most musicians had no clue about multimedia CDs. Over the course of the project, some artists dropped out and others joined the team. Each new COIN member had to get newly motivated for the project. Communication is key in such a venture, Richard explained, but communication with artists is all but easy.

Asked how he instigates new swarms, Richard explains that he always tries to brainstorm and fantasize innovations with others, preferably with people who hold opinions different from his own. He likens dreaming up new ideas to "thinking the unthinkable," exploring all the options, and leading to swarm instigation. The reality issues of what will be feasible with respect to cost, time, and skills emerge from the ensuing dialogue.

Strong-minded artists are not easy to convince to follow other people's ideas. They need to feel that new ideas are their own. Richard saw his role as an influencer, making sure that all ideas were feasible. He tried to mix everyone's ideas together. This helped forge a sense among all participants that they were working with their own ideas. When the main initiator of the multimedia concept pulled out in the middle of the project, the COIN had already become strong enough, with Richard as the main coordinator, to stay on track.

"Enhanced Gravity" delivers a perfect blueprint for coolfarming through swarm creativity based on four principles. In Table 5–1, these four principles are compared with the corresponding principles for coolhunting.

Table 5-1. Coolfarming and coolhunting.

Coolfarming	Coolhunting
Gain power by giving it away	Search for COINs and self-organizing teams
Seed community with idea	Search for ideas
Mandate intrinsic motivation	Search for intrinsically motivated people
Recruit trendsetters	Search for trendsetters

The Four Principles of Coolfarming

It may appear from Table 5–1 that these principles unfold in some linear order, but they are not necessarily sequential. They might all be applied in parallel. Let's look at each principle in detail.

1. GAIN POWER BY GIVING IT AWAY / SEARCH FOR COINS AND SELF-ORGANIZATION

The most important principle of coolfarming is to give everyone involved in the project the feeling that they have come up with the new ideas, so that all members feel a strong sense of ownership. That is precisely what Richard did when he wanted to get his fellow Dada artists to contribute their pieces of art for free to the multimedia CD. He came up with new ideas, but he took great care to convince other members of the "Enhanced Gravity" COIN that they had, in fact, invented those ideas.

Richard was by no means the first one to employ this principle. Ben Franklin stated it quite succinctly in his autobiography, when he described how he created the nation's first public subscription library. "I therefore put myself as much as I could out of sight, and stated it as a scheme of a *number of friends*, who had requested me to go about and propose it."[3] In his book on the Open Source movement, *The Cathedral and the Bazaar*, Eric Raymond describes how Linus Torvalds gives credit to his fellow Linux programmers:

> Interestingly enough, you will quickly find that if you are completely and self-deprecatingly truthful about how much you owe other people, the world at large will treat you as though you did every bit of the invention yourself and are just being becomingly modest about your innate genius. We can all see how well this worked for Linus![4]

As coolhunters, we need to look out for teams and trendsetters: the Ben Franklins and Linus Torvalds, with the personalities to create such a spirit of sharing and collaboration. Famous coolhunter and venture capitalist John Doerr of Kleiner, Perkins, Caufield & Byers is not simply looking for the next cool investment idea, but for the cool teams that display the characteristics of self-organization: They work together really well, display a high level of mutual trust, respect differences of opinion, and give credit when and to whom credit is due. When Peter's friend Wayne prospects for potential authors to write new leading-edge technical textbook, he is doing the same. He looks for the research labs that exhibit an atmosphere of intellectual freedom and individual autonomy while at the same time fostering innovative ideas and acceptance of those ideas by the academic community.

2. SEED COMMUNITY WITH AN IDEA / SEARCH FOR IDEAS

The second principle of coolfarming is to come up with the new ideas that are outside the box. This entails thinking the unthinkable, engaging others in collective brainstorming, and establishing a common vision. To develop "Enhanced Gravity," Richard tried to fantasize innovations with others, preferably with people who held opinions different than his own. This is a superb illustration of the concept of "creative chaos," where conflict is good and differing opinions are highly appreciated because they are seen as leading to progress. Philosophers throughout human history, beginning with the ancient Greeks, have understood this notion of the dialectic—the exchange of propositions and counter-propositions resulting in a qualitative transformation of the opposing assertions in a synthesis. The Socratic method is built on the dialectic; it is a practice aimed at arriving at truth through the exchange of logical arguments. Why shouldn't Richard employ such a time-honored approach?

The crucial point in a COIN is that in all of this conflict, mutual respect remains paramount. At the same time, a low-pressure environment helps people speak out about whatever crazy, new ideas might be on the table.

Coolhunter Wayne's preference is to attend academic conferences to learn about the latest trends in his fields of publishing. By talking with as many trendsetters as possible at such conferences, he forms an opinion about which inventions might become trends and open up potential markets for new textbooks. Coolhunter and Internet investor John Doerr prefers to hang out at leading universities such as Stanford, Berkeley, and MIT, where he learns about exciting new business opportunities.

Why is it that both Wayne and John Doerr find the freewheeling academic environment to be an ideal hunting and hatching ground? One reason is that in academic communities we find members with strong, intrinsic motivation—a key principle of coolfarming.

3. MANDATE INTRINSIC MOTIVATION / SEARCH FOR INTRINSICALLY MOTIVATED PEOPLE

The idea of intrinsic motivation is really about unleashing swarm creativity. A basic principle of coolfarming is to set an innovative idea free and share knowledge for free in a community. If the community accepts the new idea and the community begins to grow, the idea becomes a new trend.

Coolfarmers nurture and cultivate these trends and the trendsetters. Coolfarmers find ways to ensure that ideas are given away for free, but also to ensure that swarming takes place on the basis of intrinsic motivation and altruism. They provide everything at their disposal to potential swarms to be creative, and then they let swarm creativity happen. In a sense, they "mandate" swarms into action to create something cool.

Richard's team of "Enhanced Gravity" displays this intrinsic motivation in its purest form. All the team members joined the project because they cared about it; none of them ever expected to make any money. Nevertheless, each of the team members invested months of free sweat and labor to create a great product collaboratively.

Many academic researchers are role models of intrinsically motivated COIN members. They collaborate on creating new trends because they care about the idea, and not to get rich quickly. Robert Langer, the MIT professor who is a world leader in tissue engineering, runs a huge lab of more than 100 researchers as a COIN. They all collaborate because they care, because they want to push the cutting-edge of tissue engineering, and because they want to learn new things. Sure, it also looks good on a résumé to have worked in Langer's lab, but that's not the intrinsic motivation.

Coolfarmer Langer expects his lab members to be intrinsically motivated. Each of his post-docs has an open invitation to schedule a meeting with him anytime, but he expects them to run on their own for months at a time without close supervision. By nurturing their creativity, and by helping them to connect the dots thanks to his superior knowledge of the field, he helps them come up with cool new ideas. That way, *they* push the edge in tissue engineering, and often create innovative new startups on the way—which might then catch the interest of a coolhunter like John Doerr.

Langer's impressive portfolio of patents has led to substantial commercial success. His patents have been licensed by more than 100 pharmaceutical, chemical, biotechnology, and medical device companies. A dozen of these companies have even been started on the basis of his patents. As of our writing, his work has generated some thirty-five commercial products currently on the market, or undergoing human testing—a number sure to grow. Langer's successes are as good an indicator as any that work begun by intrinsically motivated COINs *does* lead to significant financial opportunities.

John Doerr looks out for teams like Robert Langer's, where people work together without close supervision, but also where a highly supportive environment and strong mutual respect help attract the brightest and the best, and fully unleash their creative potential. Whether it is an academic research team, the leadership team of a startup, or a new product design team for a consumer products company, these are the kinds of teams that will be setting new trends.

4. RECRUIT TRENDSETTERS / SEARCH FOR TRENDSETTERS

To create intrinsically motivated teams, teams need crystallization points in the form of leaders with the profile of a Robert Langer, a Benjamin Franklin, or a Linus Torvalds. People like Torvalds, the principle creator of Linux, or Tim Berners-Lee, the creator of the World Wide Web, have succeeded in setting trends that literally changed the world at zero budget. They are successful trendsetters who are embedded in their communities as galaxies, not as stars.

Early on, both Torvalds and Berners-Lee took on board other leaders. These intrinsically motivated individuals volunteered to take over responsibilities from the original founders. It speaks to the greatness of the original inventors of Linux and the Web that they recognized in the very early stages that they needed to give up control over their projects to ensure their success. The Web could succeed only because trendsetter Berners-Lee put himself in the background while recruiting other team members to help him carry on and develop new extensions of the Web such as Web browsers, Web servers, and Web services.

The early additions to his team exhibited characteristics similar to Berners-Lee himself: They cared deeply about the cause and not about rank, salary, and status; and they wanted to get the job done without letting money get in the way. This does not mean that they weren't compensated handsomely later on, but obviously members of the Open Source movement all could have made much more money by programming for hire than by providing their latest Web browsers and servers to the community for free. Some of these trendsetters got their rewards quite soon, however, when they caught the attention of coolhunter John Doerr, who helped them create Netscape, Amazon, and scores of other Internet startups.

In the world of rock music, we find an outstanding example of this idea of intrinsically motivated teams crystallized in the form of a leader. Readers of a certain generation may be familiar with John Mayall, the "elder statesman" of British blues. His bands, including the Bluesbreakers, are noted for being a tremendous training ground for musicians who often went on to much more acclaim than they had when playing with Mayall. One of those musicians is Eric Clapton, considered by many listeners to be among the finest rock guitarists of all time. As Clapton once said, "John Mayall has actually run an incredibly great school for musicians."

Mayall is a coolfarmer. Over four decades and forty albums, he has been centrally involved in the creation of new trends in music, nurturing and cultivating new ideas and the people who have collaborated with him to execute those ideas. Admittedly, he hasn't always been a *perfect* galaxy—perfection would have meant not making his own name part of his band's name ("John Mayall and the Bluesbreakers")—but there's no denying the tremendous role he has played as what Piero Scaruffi calls, in his excellent online rock music history, "a talent scout." Scaruffi calls the Bluesbreakers a "conveyor belt" and correctly attributes to Mayall that he "rais[ed] talents that would make the history of rock music."[5] One of the hallmarks of Mayall's coolfarming is his ability to let go of band members, who then go on to much wider fame. When the musicians he schooled in his Collaborative Innovation Network were ready to move on to bigger and better things, he usually celebrated the opportunities created for musical growth. Even the negative sentiments he expressed at the time of Eric Clapton's sudden departure from the Bluesbreakers—another small lapse in Mayall's otherwise exemplary coolfarming history—eventually gave way to support.

Through swarm creativity, John Mayall nurtured the musical innovations of an impressive—and very cool—list of musicians. In addition to the outstanding guitarists Clapton, Peter Green, and Mick Taylor—who later were part of Cream, Fleetwood Mac, and the Rolling Stones, respectively—Mayall's collaborators included John McVie and Mick Fleetwood, Aynsley Dunbar, Jack Bruce, John Almond, John Mark, Dick Heckstall-Smith, Andy Fraser, and many others. The Mark-Almond Band and Fleetwood Mac trace their origins, in important respects, to swarm creativity with John Mayall.

Think of John Mayall's Collaborative Innovation Network in business terms. Figure 5–3 shows just a small part of the Mayall galaxy. The financial implications of what Mayall's coolfarming has sown are

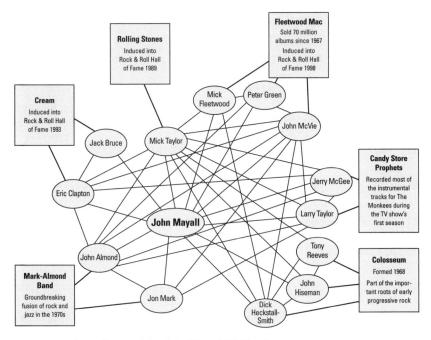

FIGURE 5–3. A small part of the John Mayall COIN galaxy.

staggering. Fleetwood Mac has sold more than 70 million records. The amount of business Eric Clapton has generated throughout the music industry, broadly defined, is probably immeasurable. Imagine your own coolfarmer galaxy spurring the kind of innovation Mayall motivated. How many trends and trendsetters, and what kind of return on investment, might you realize from "doing business" in the John Mayall way.

Given Mayall's past performance, a record label A&R guy[6] who wanted to find the next trendsetters in music couldn't do much better than to coolhunt in John Mayall's COIN. He might find the next Eric Clapton.

Let's look now at a highly successful example of coolfarming that has nothing to do with commercial success, but is all about gaining power by giving it away, nurturing cool ideas, collaborating in intrinsic motivation, and finding the right trendsetters.

A Coolfarming Example from Beyond the Business World

At Newton North High School in Newton, Massachusetts, we find an innovative theatre program under the direction of faculty member Adam Brown, who has built a remarkable community that thrives on swarm creativity. Scott's daughter is an active participant. Each school year, Theatre Ink puts up a dozen or so full-length shows—dramas, comedies, and musicals—with the participation of 300 to 400 students. High school seniors in the program direct six of the shows each school year, and there are usually three or four shows in process at any given time. Different teams work on different projects, with considerable overlap, particularly among the technical staff. The sheer volume of productions is impressive enough, but what goes on behind the scenes is even more noteworthy.

Much of the success of Theatre Ink, which bills itself as "Newton North's Working and Teaching Theatre," is linked directly to Adam. He's a coolfarmer in the best sense of the word, a trendsetter who gives power away and in doing so earns much more for himself—even though that's not what he's after. When you sit and talk with Adam, what you notice is that he hardly ever talks about himself, instead focusing on the kids and the Theatre Ink program. The seeds in his coolfarm are the students; his vision is the fertilizer; and Theatre Ink sows two great crops. One is play productions that are never worse than an "excellent high school-level production" and are often transcendent, even better than professional productions. The other is the personal growth of Newton North students involved in the program.

Adam's approach to Theatre Ink is to promote hands-on learning and empowerment. "To teach while doing," he says, "you have to give the students' ownership." How that works in Theatre Ink is a compelling example of swarm creativity. Students learn to put on shows by doing it—casting, producing, and adapting as they go.

Theatre Ink is not a class with lessons and homework. It's a holistic process in which the students are given the power to make decisions and then stick with them, learning as living.

Another aspect of the swarm in Theatre Ink is this coolfarmer's belief that "if you're in an organization, you should be able to do anything within that organization." When Adam came to Newton North, participation in theatre was smaller, and fewer students had the opportunity to be in shows. There was also more of a divide between actors and crew, who didn't necessarily see their productions as a team effort. Adam began to build a bridge between these two groups by requiring every student cast in a play to put in at least eight hours on crew during the process. Eventually, a unified community emerged, and today the crossover is remarkable. Tech kids become actors, and actors build sets and design lighting. In addition, students have learned that to earn the coveted role of director—and to be good at directing a play—they need stage management experience. Swarms of kids volunteer for backstage work.

"On high school sports teams, everyone on the team gets to practice, but at game time some students are on the bench," explains Adam. "Here, everyone's playing at game time. It's not just the actors who are players during the game, but everyone seen and unseen."

While the high school administration and academic standards have come to recognize Theatre Ink "officially" by offering a modest amount of credit towards graduation for participation by student directors and some technical theatre designers and stage crew, the hundreds of other students who participate do so simply because they want to. Except for Adam and his technical director assistant on the faculty, and five students who earn work-study pay that comes out to what Adam estimates is probably a dollar or two per hour (because of their dedication, these students work way more hours than required), no one else involved is paid a cent. They do it out of love for the theatre and love for the community Theatre Ink has created. They also care deeply about the work and what Theatre Ink brings to its audiences.

The community aspect cannot be overstated. It is a testament to the broad scope of swarm creativity involved here, and just how far-reaching the collaboration network has grown. For instance, there is a highly active parent group that supports Theatre Ink. Remarkably, the support is not just for the kids of these parents, but for the program itself—as evidenced by the parents who continue to help when their own children are not directly involved with a given production and even after their kids have graduated from high school. The amount of work done by this parent group is a significant part of what makes the program such a success. "I think that the amount of actual work these parents do is further evidence of how successful the program has been at building a shared sense of purpose and support," Adam says. "We've cultivated their commitment as much as that of the kids, and like the students they, too, produce at a high level."

If this sense of community and shared purpose continues, Adam believes, Theatre Ink will continue to thrive. And there's a lesson for life in that, he says. "Everyone wants to do something they love doing and earn a living doing it. You may not love everything about the play process or about your future job, but you have to care about it and have a passion for the overall picture. Then you'll even do the task you don't really love, gladly." It's about the whole picture.

Swarm creativity depends on three Cs, and it came as no surprise when Adam told us, with no prompting, "I'm not teaching theatre. I'm teaching *communication*, *commitment*, and *collaboration*."

How much commitment has he generated by giving power away? Consider the rigorous application and selection process involved in choosing seniors to direct the next year's shows. A committee, including the current graduating senior directors, interviews pairs of applicants who have filled out an exhaustive questionnaire not only about the play they would like to direct (which they choose), but also about how they would handle, for example, having to consider their best friends for roles. The committee evaluates their directing skills as they direct the committee members in a one-page excerpt from their proposed play. They also interview the applicants extensively. The current senior directors, even on the cusp of graduation, are heavily involved in the process, and most of them offer as much as thirty hours or more of their time without giving it a second thought. As a team, they suggest their picks for who should get to direct the following year—productions they may not even see because they'll be away at college. And Adam reports that he gets a lot of e-mails and calls the next year asking how things are going, with former students asking whether there's anything they can do and telling him how much they wish they could be at the show.

These students leave behind their legacy. Adam calls it a "Proclamation of Education" and explains: "They must not leave the space they vacate as empty, but must teach or guide someone to fill it if necessary."

Adam says those who help choose next year's shows and directors always make choices consistent with or very close to his own. "They actually help me make informed decisions," he explains, "and they come up with what's best for the program." This is very similar to the judging in swarm creativity done by the Worlddidac jurors, who subconsciously compensate for each other's "weaknesses" to serve the greater good.

One of the coolest things about Theatre Ink is how it has changed the way other Newton North faculty look at the kids involved in the theatre program. Other teachers have great respect for what Theatre Ink has accomplished, and often teachers and administrators recommend "problem" kids to the program as a way of giving them a welcoming community of which they can be a part. "In one sense, many staff members look at Theatre Ink kids differently," Adam explains. "They're no longer just the kids who come to math class, but now they're seen as kids who do their math *and* put in all this other time. It gives other teachers a more holistic picture of the kids."

Above all else, Theatre Ink isn't just cool; it brings kids of all ages and backgrounds together. It's a place students can come to cultivate themselves. If they are willing to walk in the door and take some risks, they can join in at any time, find something to connect to, and they will inevitably make friends and become part of the community.

Parents and students alike help to promote and sustain the program by investing themselves and getting others to invest. It works because of swarm creativity, and Theatre Ink exhibits nearly every principle of swarm creativity. It also works because of a coolfarmer who cultivates the swarm to create innovation every day.

"I challenge you to walk around other groups of high school students in a swarm, and find this level of conversation, commitment, and community," says Adam. "It's beyond cool here."

Coolfarming That Truly Changed the World: Netscape

Turning our attention again to the business world, consider the cutting-edge tale of the first widely used Web browser. The story of Netscape, and its protagonists Jim Clark and Marc Andreesen, illustrates the power of coolfarming.

Dr. James H. Clark, a computer scientist described by one journalist as a "serial entrepreneur,"[7] is the founder of several Silicon Valley technology companies. While a professor of electrical engineering at Stanford University in the late 1970s, he and his students developed the Geometry Engine, an early technology for displaying three-dimensional images. Clark's research is credited as one of the important milestones in allowing fast rendering of computer images, today ubiquitous on the World Wide Web.

Just as the World Wide Web began to take off, a young student and part-time assistant at the National Center for Supercomputing Applications (NCSA) at the University of Illinois began to develop a browser. The student's name was Marc Andreesen. Most of the available browsers were for Unix machines, which were very expensive and most accessible to engineers and academics. The browsers were also less than "user-friendly," with difficult inter-faces and rather poor graphics. Andreesen set out to create some-thing better.

Andreesen recruited an NCSA employee named Eric Bina to help. They worked feverishly and developed a new browser, which they called Mosaic. Its graphics—rich and sophisticated—were like nothing else available. Mosaic also included new formatting tags in Hypertext Markup Language (HTML), further expanding its use-fulness. And it included an "image" tag that made it possible to include text and images on the same Web page, which was a dra-matic improvement over the existing protocol that allowed viewing of pictures but only as separate files.

These innovations of Andreesen and Bina, and others in that first release of Mosaic are things we take for granted today. Mosaic had a graphical interface with clickable buttons that allowed users to navigate with ease. There were controls that let users scroll through text. And Mosaic replaced the old reference numbers that users of earlier browsers had to type in to navigate to a linked document with hyperlinks—simple clicking on a link to retrieve a document.

In early 1993, the Unix version of Mosaic was posted for free download on NCSA's servers, and within weeks tens of thousands of people were using the browser. Andreesen and Bina quickly teamed with others to develop versions for PCs and Macintosh computers, and by late spring Mosaic was driving the creation of a massive community of Web users through these more popular platforms. The Web began to explode: More users meant more content, which in turn attracted more users. Everyone wanted to use Mosaic, which had spurred this growth.

These young men had done something extraordinary and important. As the *New York Times* reported that December, in a lead article in its daily Business section, "Mosaic's many passionate proponents hail it as the first 'killer app' of network computing—an applications program so different and so obviously useful that it can create a new industry from scratch."[8] Andreesen and Bina had truly changed the world. "There are two ages of the Internet—before Mosaic, and after. . . . In twenty-four months, the Web has gone from being unknown to absolutely ubiquitous."[9] Notably, the *Times* article failed to mention either Andreesen or Bina by name, referring only to NCSA. Andreesen, realizing that NCSA would be taking over his creation, graduated and moved on to California's Silicon Valley. He took a job at a company that developed Internet security products.

It wasn't long before Andreesen received an e-mail from Jim Clark, who had long since left academia. In the intervening period, he had founded Silicon Graphics, Inc—a company that made him a millionaire. Clark had taken the technology he had invented and converted it into a highly successful business. He had already shown himself to be a successful coolfarmer. When Clark and Andreesen met, Clark had left Silicon Graphics and was looking for a new venture.

The two men talked a lot about technology, and in their discussions Andreesen told Clark that 25 million people were using the

Internet. Whether Clark had already honed in on Andreesen's browser for his new business venture, or whether the discussions revealed the path, Clark saw the potential, and he and Andreesen decided to go into business together. They founded an Internet company called Mosaic Communications Corporation in mid-1994.[10] Their business objective was to create a product that would surpass the original Mosaic browser. And they had to start from the beginning, because the University of Illinois owned the original, which had been created on its time and with its money.

In another sign of coolfarming, the new company convinced several of Andreesen's friends from NCSA to move from Illinois to California and comprise Mosaic Communications Corp.'s engineering team. The new company, under Jim Clark's leadership, recruited the trendsetters.

It didn't take long for these geniuses to create a new product, which they called Netscape.[11] Clark developed a pricing structure. At first, he planned to charge $99 for the browser, $5,000 for the basic server, and $25,000 for the commercial server (which included a technology for encrypting sensitive information such as credit card numbers). But he reconsidered and decided to charge $1,500 for the baseline server and $5,000 for the commercial server. But the development team—the Collaborative Innovation Network that had created Netscape—knew better. Mosaic had been given away for free, and they knew that Netscape would succeed by being everywhere on the Web. "That was the way to get the company jump-started, because that just gives you essentially a broad platform to build off of," Andreesen later remarked.[12] Clark paid heed to the people in the company who were swarming together creatively—a good sign that he was a skilled coolfarmer. He agreed to a pricing structure they called "free but not free"—the Netscape browser would be given away at no charge to students and teachers, but everyone else would have to pay $39. But Netscape really was free for all, because every new Beta version—which were continuous, as the development team made continual improvements—was downloadable, and the current version could be tried for 90 days at no charge. The company rarely enforced the trial period. The only real revenue came from the version that could be purchased by mail and from the servers.

Clark didn't worry, though, because he came to believe what Andreesen already knew—that power could be gained by giving the product away. They looked for other ways to fund their efforts, such as by selling advertising on the company's home page. And within weeks of its October 1994 launch, Netscape had become the browser of choice for most Web users. Excited designers quickly began incorporating the new tags into their pages. As with its predecessor, Mosaic, this drove Web improvements, which in turn drove more use of Netscape. Designers used the new HTML tags, which could be read only by Netscape, so they would include a statement on their Web pages that users should download Netscape for "best viewing."

The initial public offering of Netscape shares in August 1995 is often cited as the beginning of the dot-com stock market frenzy (admittedly a rather dubious honor, as we discuss in Chapter 6). It was one of the most successful share offerings in U.S. history. The stock went from $28 to $72 on opening day, and the young engineers at Netscape became rich from their stock options. Marc Andreesen, a mere twenty-four years old, was suddenly worth $80 million. Clark's business model had cemented the stock option as a regular feature of technology company hirings.

While the Netscape company faced many travails later on, and today is something rather different from what it was in its early days, the story of Andreesen's Netscape COIN and coolfarmer Jim Clark is tremendously instructive. It is a strong illustration of a particular kind of "giving power away" in the world of software. The Netscape executives understood that putting the browser in the hands of millions of users would create a demand for the company's secondary product—its software for Web servers. By creating a huge market of potential users, they hoped to convince content providers to use Netscape's server products. Additionally, just by providing a spot on the Web where millions of users could get their browsers for free, they succeeded in making their site one of the hottest properties on the Web. By sharing its main product for free, Netscape succeeded in creating a large secondary market for its supporting products: the Web server and its Web address.

This insight into sharing knowledge and giving power away has been widely copied. For instance, their makers gave away software such as Real Player for free to millions, which created the demand for content and the need for content providers to purchase the streaming audio and video servers from Real Networks. The player drove the market for a secondary product, and users were the ones in the driver's seat. Bill Gates used the same insight to leverage his huge base of Microsoft Windows users to grab away market share from Netscape in the infamous browser wars during the height of the e-business bubble.

We think this really is giving a kind of power away. It's not the same as the tactic of giving away a sample—like at the grocery store—in an effort to hook the consumer and build future sales of the product. And it's different from the much-touted business strategy of Gillette, to give away the razor and sell the blades. In these examples, the consumer ultimately pays.

It's hard to imagine a world in which Microsoft would have offered the initial release of a Web browser for free if it hadn't been forced to do so by the dominant business model of Netscape—which Bill Gates sought to crush—to gain power by giving browsers away for free.

Netscape thrived for a long time because it functioned like a galaxy. Of course, not all coolfarming stories have happy endings. Sometimes those who try to do coolfarming ignore the principles of collaboration and open communication that are so critical to success—and they end up failing miserably.

Coolfarming Gone Wrong: Boo.com

Consider the case of Boo.com, founded in 1998 in England by three Swedish entrepreneurs during the dot-com heyday. Ernst Malmsten, Kajsa Leander, and Patrik Hedelin had a vision: They would build the world's first retail fashion website with a hip European brand image that would appeal globally to 18-to-24-year-old consumers with disposable income. They wanted their site to be, to the greatest degree possible, an online version of a real-life shopping experience.

The website was definitely unique, employing all kinds of technological wizardry that less than a decade later we take for granted, but was quite rare for the time. The site was built using Java and Flash programming that allowed buyers to select products, drag them to "human" models, and then zoom in and rotate the models in 3D to get a picture of what the item would look like when worn. There was Miss Boo, the virtual salesperson who guided users through the site and offered helpful shopping tips. There was even an online magazine, *Boom*. The Boo.com site required a huge amount of bandwidth.

Investors loved this idea. Venture capitalists and others forked over nearly $120 million in a very short period to develop the technology and get Boo.com launched for consumers. The big-name backers included investment banks J.P. Morgan and Goldman Sachs, fashion retailer Benetton, as well as Bernard Arnault, chairman of the global conglomerate Louis Vuitton Moët Hennessy—the self-described "world leader in luxury."

It took a mere six months for the company to burn through this money. And Boo.com has gone down in the annals of e-commerce as Europe's first major dot-com failure.

Analysts point to many reasons for Boo.com's demise. There was the six-month delay in launching the site, which cost it a lot of lost revenue. When Boo.com finally did launch, shoppers found it a difficult site to navigate: "Shoppers found themselves confused, even driven away, by the cartoon salespeople and cumbersome design of the oh-so-hip online shop."[13] But we think the lesson of Boo.com's failure is best told in terms of coolfarming and swarm creativity.

Tristan Louis worked for the ill-fated Boo.com but left before its demise. On his website he points to "lack of communications to and from the top" and notes that "management makes or breaks a company."[14] Boo.com was all about creating trends, but it was a failed coolfarmer. From all the press reports, it's pretty clear that for all its speed in spending its venture capital, management was very slow—perhaps even inert—in getting together an intrinsically motivated group of movers and shakers. Boo.com failed to nurture and cultivate the new ideas from its talented employees that would have sustained the site and, perhaps, turned it into the success everyone expected. Busy trying to do coolhunting on the outside and selling its customers on cool trends, it failed to do coolfarming on the inside.

If anything good came out of the Boo.com debacle, it may be the company's inability to raise an additional $30 million from investors in its last, dying days. While there had been an initial frenzy among investors to get in on the ground floor, the refusal to pump more funds in as the ship was sinking is the opposite of a phenomenon we see all too often—the collective madness of swarms, especially when it looks like there's money to be made (even if it's "too good to be true"). The whole dot-com collapse speaks to this, which is the subject of our next chapter.

6

When Swarms Go Mad

We find that whole communities suddenly fix their minds upon one object, and go mad in its pursuit; that millions of people become simultaneously impressed with one delusion, and run after it, till their attention is caught by some new folly more captivating than the first.

—Charles Mackay[1]

THUS FAR, we've focused on the swarm being right, which is usually the case—a crowd of people is smarter than the smartest individual expert, many times. Swarms easily outperform the single, bright mind, not only when it comes to guessing the weight of a slaughtered ox or answering the types of questions asked on *Who Wants to Be a Millionaire?* but also for business-critical tasks, such as making a sales forecast, creating a new computer operating system, or determining which movie might be a big hit at the box office. There are, however, plenty of examples of the swarm being very wrong.

Collective Madness

Some of the examples are horrifying. For instance, all notions of justice and due process fly out the window once a lynch mob is on the loose. Even entire nations can go awry, and we don't need to go back very far to find examples. Swarms of people participated in the massacres in Rwanda that began on April 6, 1994, and continued for the next 100 days or so. Up to 800,000 Tutsis were killed by Hutu militia using clubs and machetes. On some days, human rights experts suggest, as many as 10,000 were slaughtered. In the republics of the former Yugoslavian federation, swarms of people bought into government lies about their ethnically different neighbors; at worst, they participated in mass killings, and at best they turned a blind eye as people were dragged away. Of course, there's the Holocaust carried out by the Nazis. In the swarm, unfortunately, delusion—the erroneous belief held in the face of strong evidence to the contrary—can seem to take on a life of its own. In the realm of business and economics, we can find plenty of examples, too. While the results aren't the same as the massacres just mentioned, the lessons are similar.

THE MISSISSIPPI SCHEME

Take the swarm behavior during economic bubbles. There are well-documented instances throughout history where millions of people seem to have lost any "business sense" and began to speculate madly until the bubble burst and made many people a lot poorer. The so-called Mississippi Scheme of the early eighteenth century is a prime example. In August 1717, a Scottish businessman by the name of John Law acquired a controlling interest in a bankrupt firm called the Mississippi Company, renamed it *Compagnie d'Occident*, and set out to do business with the French colonies in North America. At the time, the French controlled much of the Mississippi River delta and, of course, Louisiana. Law succeeded in getting the French regent, Philippe II, *duc d'Orléans*, to sanction his plan.

Within two years, Law had monopoly control over French colonial trade, his company having absorbed several others established for developing the Indies, China, and Africa. The consolidated firm, renamed Compagnie des Indes, was commonly known as the Mississippi Company, and enjoyed all sorts of privileges from the French crown—even rights to taxation. Soon, the company assumed the state debt and, in 1720, was merged with France's royal bank.

These moves spurred such public confidence in the company that its shares became the object of a wild orgy of speculation. Law promoted the orgy with advertising that described Louisiana as a land full of mountains nearly bursting with gold and silver—an obvious lie to anyone who has ever visited there, but accepted by swarming French investors. What finally brought an end to Law's scheme was the overexpansion of the Mississippi Company's activities coupled with a nearly complete lack of any genuine assets in the colonies. While a few speculators were able to get out in time, with huge profits, the overwhelming majority were ruined when the bubble burst in October 1720. This caused a governmental crisis in France, and by December of that year Law had to flee the country. The only remnant of the Mississippi Scheme in Louisiana is the large number of descendants of the big influx of French settlers who uprooted their lives and traveled to the region, incited by Law's false advertising.

TULIP MANIA

Another example has even given a name to the phenomenon of a large economic bubble: tulip mania, or tulipomania. It is a reference to a major financial crisis in the Netherlands only a few decades after the tulip—today so closely associated with Holland—

was introduced to the region and became a status symbol among the prosperous Dutch.

In 1636, the tulip had become so popular that the demand for bulbs was enormous. People began to use the tulip for speculation, and would go into enormous debt to buy tulip bulbs at very high prices and then sell them at an even higher price. How high did prices go? A single bulb at the time could fetch as much as a big house in a prime location.

By 1637, the States of Holland were compelled to pass a statute that curbed the extremes associated with tulip prices and tulip speculation. This finally burst the bubble that had enveloped otherwise sensible people and compelled them to behave so irrationally. It was another example of overheated speculation that gave us the word "bubble" to associate with this irrational swarm behavior.

THE SOUTH SEA COMPANY STOCK BUBBLE

In 1711, The South Sea Company was formed in England and was granted exclusive trading right in Spanish South America. The government traded these rights for what it thought would be tremendous profits from convincing investors holding some £10 million of short-term government debt to exchange those papers with newly issued South Sea Company stock. The deal was structured to "guarantee" the new equity owners a steady stream of earnings in the new company.

Things didn't go so well, and the company's trading business largely floundered. But the company continued to argue that the long-term picture was extremely good, and even traded equity for more public debt. By 1719, The South Sea Company was proposing a scheme in which it would purchase a whopping portion of Britain's national debt—more than half!—and convert the debt to a lower interest rate so that everyone could win with the ability to sell more attractive, more readily marketable paper. The Bank of England proposed a different buyout, but the company raised its offer and prevailed.

Then came the swarm madness. First the company began to float outrageous rumors about the potential value of its trades in the New World. This set off a frenzy of speculation, with share prices skyrocketing from £128 in January 1720, when the scheme was first proposed, to £550 at the end of May, when the government signed on to the debt buyout. Meanwhile, the company was "paying off" politicians with shares in another scheme where Members of Parliament, government ministers, and even the King's mistress were given shares that they could then "sell" back to the company and receive as "profit" the increase in market price. The decision-makers involved found themselves in cahoots with the company in a unique way: they weren't just taking what amounted to bribes, but to secure their own profits they had to help drive the stock price up. The South Sea Company, meanwhile, made sure the general investor public knew about all these high-ranking, elite shareholders; after all, it made the company look good.

Not surprisingly, other speculators began to see the short-term value in a joint-stock scheme like this and joined the market with new companies—nicknamed "bubbles"—that also were based on fraudulent claims or exotic money-making schemes.

When the price of South Sea Company stock began to approach the £1000-per-share mark, citizens across the British Isles and from every imaginable socio-economic stratum, began to see investing as something worth getting into. Purchasing shares in the many companies that sprouted up became a national pastime—with little thought put into the investment. One company that went public in 1720 advertised itself as one "for carrying out an undertaking of great advantage, but nobody to know what it is." And still people invested!

In early August 1720, the magic £1000-per-share mark was hit, and there was so much selling that the price began to plummet. By the end of the year, it was back to £100, and people who had bought shares on credit were going bankrupt everywhere. Around the same time, payments on the early issues of South Sea Stock were coming due, and the company didn't have the money to meet its obligations. The bubble burst—around the same time as John Law's Mississippi Scheme in France was collapsing.

Much more recently, in 1996, the Albanian economy underwent a cataclysmic illustration of swarm madness.[2] As the nation was transitioning from a planned to a market economy, a handful of so-called deposit-taking companies emerged and promised to invest funds for Albanian citizens. In truth, though, it was a pyramid scheme that relied on new participants "investing" money that would then go to those who had "invested" before them, in an ever-narrowing hierarchy all the way up to the top of the pyramid.

A pyramid scheme generates income only by promising high returns on investment to those who get involved—returns that can be paid only if new investors are recruited. Eventually, the pyramid must collapse. It's a simple mathematics issue: There is a finite number of potential investors.

The Albanian pyramid was truly devastating. No less than two-thirds of the country's population invested, desperate for some way out of the deprivation they had suffered under decades of Stalinist rule by a privileged caste. They divested themselves of livestock, homes, and furniture to raise money to put into the scheme. Total investments equaled half of the country's total gross domestic product.

When it all came tumbling down in late 1996 and early 1997, Albania's gross national product fell to minus 7 percent. The country erupted into anarchy; tens of thousands fled the land; and civilian militias emerged to protect what little assets were still in people's hands—and to hunt down the people who had started the pyramid. The death toll hit 2,000.

DOT-COMS GO BUST

The implosion of the dot-com bubble between 1997 and 2001 may well be the most famous example in the very recent past. Internet-based startups—called dot-coms—were multiplying like flies, fueled by venture capitalists who seemed to have thrown common business sense out the window. Detailed business plans that defined a steady set of growth steps were abandoned in getting on the bandwagon, and once the startups were open for business the abandonment of common sense in favor of unchecked exuberance seemed to continue unabated. Market share became the mantra, and money was thrown at whatever strategy or tactic looked on a given day as if it might produce market share—regardless of the bottom-line impact.

The bandwagon extended beyond the venture capitalists to attract other investors. Dot-coms made Initial Public Offerings of stock, often before they had produced a single product or generated even $1.00 in revenue. Yet, their stock prices rose rapidly and speculation ran rampant. Soon, the bubble burst, even sparking a recessionary period in the Western economies. Several of the "promising" Internet-based startups became rather spectacular failures.

So much has been written in detail about this, and we don't want to revisit what has become such common knowledge. But one point in particular is worth mentioning—call it the "ripple effect" of dot-com madness. Sometimes the "irrational exuberance" of the investors swarming to pump money into ventures incites a kind of internal swarm madness within the venture itself.

Webvan.com was a California-based dot-com founded in the late 1990s as an online grocery shopping site. The business model is one that has outlasted the dot-com bubble, and today there are successful online grocers in a number of regions of the United States. Webvan, though, failed because of its own internal swarm madness. It was run by executives who shared a notable characteristic with its major investors: they had zero experience in the supermarket industry. It tried to do everything on its own, without any connections to existing "bricks-and-mortar" grocers or a supermarket chain or to a food supplier. It tried to expand very, very quickly, based on its initial popularity with consumers. But the real madness was in how Webvan spent money far in excess of its sales to build its infrastructure, including purchasing "at least 115 Herman Miller Aeron chairs (at over \$800 each)."[3] Webvan failed to tap into swarm creativity—the kind where it might have learned something from people who knew something about the grocery business. Instead, "the most audacious and second-best-financed attempt to rewrite the rules of retailing came to an abrupt end."[4]

□   □   □

Just what is it that gets people to participate in collective madness? As you will see, the boundary between madness and wisdom is frequently rather narrow. Understanding what gets people to cross that boundary is a double valuable lesson for the purpose of coolhunting. On the one hand, looking at what went wrong when large groups of people swarmed together for the greater good can teach us how to do things better. For that lesson, we'll look first at the Columbia space shuttle disaster. On the other hand, crowds gone wrong often exhibit strong similarities with Collaborative Innovation Networks (COINs). If we suspect that something is going wrong, or has gone wrong within a community, that a swarm has crossed the boundary to the bad, we can apply the coolhunting principles we developed earlier to hunt for suspicious patterns. To illustrate this idea, we look later in this chapter at what went wrong with Enron, and how coolhunting could have been applied early on to uncover the swarming madness and warn potential investors.

Lack of Open Communication
Can Be Fatal: NASA

COINs function with open, honest communication. Ideas are judged on their merits, not on the basis of one's hierarchical position. These are essential aspects of COINs—and they can mean the difference between success and failure in the innovation process. Without open, honest communication, the ability of people who are otherwise tremendously innovative can be shut at the very moment when their brainpower might be most needed. The business results can be fatal for a project; in some cases, the fatalities can be even worse.

Consider the U.S. National Aeronautics and Space Administration (NASA). No one could argue that the NASA scientists and engineers lack the innovator's "gene." In fact, the agency was created for the very purpose of innovation. NASA scientists and engineers operate swarm intelligence. But, as the tragedy of the Space Shuttle Columbia illustrates, NASA's innovative capabilities are severely hampered by rigid "command and control" structures that keep it from being a genuine COIN. Open and honest communication is buried in NASA's huge hierarchy.

Were it not for the culture of NASA, the Columbia disaster might not have happened. This is not our conclusion, but the result of an in-depth look at NASA by the *New York Times*.[5] On February 1, 2003, Columbia disintegrated during reentry into the Earth's atmosphere, after a 16-day mission. The entire seven-member crew died. It was quickly established that a hole blasted at takeoff into the leading edge of the left wing by a piece of foam was technically responsible for the damage that caused the crash, another main culprit was only identified much later: NASA's rigid management culture.

Like most conventional, hierarchical organizations, NASA had a hard time accepting this verdict. Top management focused on technical matters, immediately implementing five technical criteria established by a panel of investigators to improve future shuttle flights. The management culture issue was largely swept under the rug. When Bill Readdy, NASA's associate administrator for space flight, was asked at a press conference about whether NASA would reevaluate it's culture, he said, "The comment that it's a culture thing maybe does apply in some small area." And then, adopting a consummately defensive posture, he reminded reporters that it was NASA's strong culture that "got us to the Moon, and got us back to the mission."[6] The New York Times painted a devastating picture of communication—or, more accurately—of the lack of communication at NASA.[7] A flurry of e-mail messages showed that several NASA engineers around the country wanted spy satellite images of the affected wing once the problem had been noticed after launch. One made an informal request that NASA officially withdrew, and a top official at the agency's headquarters actually turned down an offer of help from an Air Force surveillance agency. Even when NASA staff engineer Paul Shack pointed out the risk of the piece of foam seven days before the crash, the agency did not take the issue of debris seriously and failed to follow through on the first impulses of other NASA engineers to get pictures of the shuttle in orbit. While Columbia was in orbit, Linda Ham, the leader of the NASA ground team, heard that there had been a request for spy satellite images and tried to find out why; she wasn't told by officials about the risk assessment of Shack and others.

The NASA example is a prime negative example of how even a tremendously innovative organization can fail to be a COIN and capture all the benefits that come from working in a truly collaborative way. Investigators determined that the agency's work culture discouraged dissenting views on safety issues. Information did not flow in the ways it needed to, and the NASA approach to peer review and accountability prohibited its own engineers from following their instincts. External contractors that the agency relied on for some of the deep technical analysis needed to make space flight successful were afraid to speak out clearly—a phenomenon known in the contractor community as "NASA chicken syndrome." In short, NASA contractors and employees alike were afraid to stick their necks out. They were reluctant to raise any flags that would slow down a project and might carry political or economic risks. Instead, they bided their time, hoping that others would speak up.

As the *Times* reported, one NASA engineer explained, "The NASA culture does not accept being wrong." It is not a culture where "there's no such thing as a stupid question" but one where "the humiliation factor always runs high."[8] Had NASA adopted a more open and more meritocratic culture of self-responsibility—like we find in real Collaborative Innovation Networks—Linda Ham might have gotten the answer she was looking for in time to do something about Columbia's fractured left wing. The accident might not have happened, and seven astronauts might still be alive.

After investigations of the accident, which included a hard look inside NASA's organizational culture, reports were issued and recommendations were made. Finally, the NASA senior leadership admitted the problem. Speaking at a press conference on April 14, 2004, after briefing NASA personnel on the plans to change the agency from a "can-do" culture to one that puts safety first, NASA Administrator Sean O'Keefe said, "We need to create a climate in which open communication is not only permissible but is actively encouraged."[9] In a COIN, open communication is not only actively encouraged, but is a central part of what makes the network one of genuinely *collaborative* innovation. What really matters is that open communication be a part of the corporate culture, not just something to which management pays lip service. Enron is a prime example of a company that seemed to do everything right from the outside, including declaring an open communication policy. As it turned out, however, it was entirely rotten from the inside.

Egomania at Enron

In its heyday, Enron was one of the world's leading energy, commodities, and services firms. The company marketed electricity and natural gas, delivered energy and other physical commodities, and provided financial and risk management services to customers around the world. It was seen as the corporate high flyer of the 1990s, one of the best and most innovative companies in the world. Enron's 1998 annual report set some lofty corporate goals:

- *"Respect:* We treat others as we would like to be treated ourselves . . ."

- *"Integrity:* We work with customers and prospects openly, honestly, and sincerely ..."

- *"Communication:* We have an obligation to communicate: Here, we take the time to talk with one another ..."

- *"Excellence:* We are satisfied with nothing less than the very best in everything we do. We will continue to raise the bar for everyone. The great fun here will be for all of us to discover just how good we really can be."[10]

As it put forward this public face, the company's real behavior was corruption, with its executives consumed by greed.

A quick peek behind the scenes exposes the four behavioral guidelines set out in the 1998 annual report as hypocrisies of the highest order. Take "respect." Despite its vaunted pledge, Enron became infamous and feared for the high-handed behavior of its executives in its dealings with utility companies, who were its business partners and whose energy it was selling.

The second statement about "integrity" is nothing if not breathtaking in its brazenness. Enron really had just one goal, and that was to meet the expectations of Wall Street. This meant accounting rules were bent with unabashed boldness. Integrity was flushed down the drain.

No less ignored was the idea that Enron would "communicate" openly. The company purposefully fostered a kind of dog-eat-dog internal competition by hiding information not only from the outside, but even within its own ranks. There are many well-documented instances where two managers from different Enron business units would appear at a client site and fight—right in front of the customer—for the same deal.

In light of the principles of creativity and collaboration, the last goal—"excellence"—stands out in particular. A commitment to excellence by being the "best" should raise warning signals.

Enron managers considered themselves "the smartest guys in the room."[11] This culture was reinforced by the heritage brought from McKinsey & Company to Enron by Jeffrey Skilling, the company's chief operating officer and, for a brief period, chief executive officer. Skilling filled the management offices of Enron with former McKinsey partners and consultants.

McKinsey & Company is a management consulting firm founded in 1926. The focus of the firm's corporate culture is the superiority of brain and intellect over "softer" emotional and cultural values. As McKinsey's former managing director Ron Daniel once told *Fortune* magazine, the firm looks "to hire people who are, first, very smart; second, insecure, and thus driven by their insecurity; and third competitive. Put together 3,000 of these egocentric, task-oriented, achievement-oriented people, and it produces an atmosphere of something less than humility. Yes, it's elitist."[12] Skilling helped transfer this corporate culture to Enron, and then reinforced it until Enron's sense of pride was based on having the highest accumulated intellect in its industry. Humility, modesty, and the recognition that there might be others who could be more knowledgeable, who might even be smarter, and from whom Enron could possibly learn became ideas entirely alien to Enron management and culture.

A Collaborative Innovation Network thrives on swarm creativity. Sometimes, though, what looks like a COIN is not really a COIN, and what appears to be swarm creativity may actually be swarm destruction. In its obsession with being the "smartest guys in the room," Enron deviated tremendously from swarm creativity. Enron applied its accumulated swarm intelligence to optimizing profits and beating Wall Street's expectation. This wasn't swarm creativity, but swarm arrogance—and in the end Enron destroyed itself.

What a COIN and a Religious Cult Have in Common: "The Family"

There are some strong similarities between religious cults and COIN-like communities. There is not that much difference between Enron executives worshiping smart guys making loads of money and members of a religious cult worshipping "god" through their cult leaders. There's nothing inherently wrong with leaders who are viewed by the community in a "cult-like" way—so long as the leader's values and behavior are consistent with a true COIN. Consider, for instance, Linus Torvalds, regarded as the undisputed leader of the Linux movement while at the same time he was giving power away, or Steve Jobs, who was coordinating an innovative galaxy that created Apple computers and the iPod.

A negative example of a close-knit COIN-like community can be found in the religious cult "The Family."[13] You may well ask what a religious cult has to do with collaborative innovation. From the point of view of creativity, the invention of the light bulb and the idea for a new religion both claim to make the world a better place. For starters, the members of this religious cult—like others—honestly believe that their collaboration is in the service of making a better world. For this very reason, the behavior within some religious cults—especially those of the communal sort—can bear striking similarities to COINs. Religious cults like The Family are often self-organized and function with swarm intelligence. They establish themselves with egalitarian principles, following the scriptural proclamation that God is impartial when it comes to people.[14] What they usually lack, though, is transparency and meritocracy. These differences between religious cults and true COINs teach a valuable lesson for how swarm creativity can succeed in a business context.

The Family, today calling itself Family International, was established in 1968 in Huntington Beach, California, and drew quite a few of its early converts from hippies who were looking for a place to live communally in the "true mode" of Christianity.

David Berg, the cult's founder, set as the group's mission to witness and save souls for Jesus throughout the world, and he saw his followers as God's elite "End Time Army." He came up with an innovative approach to fueling his vision and winning converts. Members of The Family saw "Father David," who died in 1994, as a chosen prophet. He established "the System"—a message of salvation, apocalypticism, and collective concentration of energy and resources to carry out the End Time mission. What might seem perverse to us resonated with his followers. The Family's separation from society, communal approach to living, norm of sexual sharing within the group, and "Flirty Fishing"—a method of evangelism that used sex to "show God's love" and win converts—have all fueled The Family's controversial status and kept it in persistent tension with society as it has grown around the world.

Like a multinational corporation, The Family does operate in many ways like a global collaboration network. It makes heavy use of the Internet and relies on e-mail for most of its global communication. The cult's basic governing document, "The Family Charter," details a system of governance for individual homes organized around the concepts of teamwork, leadership, and democratic participation in decision making. The group has different categories of membership that reflect a range of different commitment levels. You can be a member who has made a contractual commitment to obey all The Family's fundamental rules and responsibilities; you might be in the process of meeting the membership requirements; or you might simply make financial contributions. The different levels of membership reflect the same kinds of roles we have found people playing in other COINs.

After Father David's death, The Family developed a new planning and policy-making system called "The Board Vision" to expand the group's leadership, distributing leadership tasks among some 500 "Charter Members" (the highest membership level) on six boards to create greater efficiency in carrying out its central evangelizing mission. The boards are organized around six central areas of concern that are considered essential for the Family's continued growth and vitality: parenting young children, guiding teen youths, home schooling for both children and teens, church growth and missionary outreach programs, supervision and visitation of Family Homes, and public relations. And it is here where we find the main difference between The Family and a COIN.

The Board Vision represents a corporate model of organizational decision making and control under the centralized authority and direction of Maria and Peter, who became the leaders of The Family after Father David's death. It is a striking elaboration of bureaucratic administration in a religion whose conviction that it is being led through daily direct supernatural communication with Jesus Christ and the spiritual world is extraordinary. Contrary to a COIN, the Family requests unconditional obedience from its followers and does not shy away from enforcing its rules by policing members. For instance, a call from Maria and Peter required all Charter Members age 16 and older worldwide either to sign a contract pledging their faith and willingness to live up to the group's standards or leave The Family altogether.

More recently, in 2004, the Family was again reorganized, refining membership levels and further cementing the spiritual leadership of Maria and Peter.[15] In prayer and consultation with expanded leadership, Maria and Peter claim final unquestioning authority. Family members are explicitly asked to maintain faith in Father David as God's End Time Prophet and in Maria and Peter as Father David's anointed successors.

As with Enron, swarm creativity turned horribly wrong for The Family. The Family's teachings have led to a horrible murder-suicide,[16] where Maria's grown-up son murdered one of his former nannies and then took his own life. One website points to at least twenty-five other children reared by The Family who have taken their own lives since the early 1990s. By demanding unquestioning authority for their teachings from their followers, Maria and Peter display the same arrogance as Enron's leadership did, turning swarm creativity into swarm destruction.

On the surface, The Family and Enron both displayed strong, common behavioral codes whose ingrained values of integrity, open communication, and meritocracy should have made them exemplary Collaborative Innovation Networks, working together in swarm creativity. In reality, however, these values were mere lip service, and their true shared DNA ran counter to all the characteristics of swarm creativity. Anything their executives said in support of collaboration was insincere at best, and we can see where it led. Nevertheless, they teach a great lesson of where swarm creativity can lead if it is corrupted.

Both Enron and The Family created cool trends—at least for their followers. Members of The Family were embedded in a loving community that gave a new sense of importance to their lives. Enron managers enjoyed stellar financial success. In the end, though, following those trends led to Enron's destruction and deep misery for numerous children of The Family.

What can we learn from all those instances where swarm creativity turned into collective madness? Obviously, greed is often stronger than reason. Tulip mania, the South Sea bubble, and the e-business bubble just a few years ago all show people discarding common sense. Like lemmings, they steered towards the abyss, convincing each other that their madness was rational. They followed people they considered "cool," but those trendsetters were no Ben Franklins. They were egomaniacs, like the Enron executives. They were cult leaders, like the "prophets" of The Family. They pretended to be altruistic and to act for the common good, but ultimately their only real interest was in increasing their own material wealth and power.

Use the bees from Chapter 2 as a benchmark. Unlike in the beehive, there is nary a spark of altruism in these two examples. There is nothing but selfishness. It is the same in the pyramid scheme.

Swarm creativity advances us as people; swarm madness—so often predicated on selfishness—sets us back. It's an extraordinarily valuable business lesson. As Isaac Asimov, who inspired us to go beyond purely intuitive coolhunting, wrote:

The wisdom of mankind will never improve the material lot of man unless advancing knowledge presents it with the matters over which it can make those decisions. And when, despite the most careful decisions, there come dangerous side effects of the new knowledge—it is only still further advances in knowledge that will offer hope for correction.[17]

The patterns displayed in the examples of Enron and The Family are very similar to the patterns of *real* COINs, but the motivations of those involved have nothing to do with collaborative innovation and swarm creativity. Nevertheless, they show that the same principles and tools that can be applied to hunt for cool trends developed in swarm creativity can also be used to uncover collective madness.

Let's now explore further how you can use patterns of swarm creativity for coolhunting both good and bad trends.

7

Do-It-Yourself Coolhunting with Technology

As technology advances, it reverses the characteristics of every situation again and again. The age of automation is going to be the age of "do it yourself."

—Marshall McLuhan (1957)[1]

THE WEB offers a great environment for anyone who wants to hunt for trends. Examples abound: myriad newsgroups, community websites (Yahoo groups, tribe.net, etc.), lists of the "most e-mailed articles" (such as from the *New York Times*), lists of the most frequently bought books on Amazon, moderated news websites such as Wikinews, and blogs such as Slashdot, boingboing, and technorati. At times, it seems as if the sources on the Web for coolhunting trends are limitless.

Before any "non-techies" get nervous, it's important to realize that not all coolhunting on the Web requires cutting-edge technology.

There are plenty of "low-tech" ways to coolhunt online. We find a great example among members of a church congregation in the Boston area and their need for dental care.

When a member of the church needed a new dentist, he posted his request on the local congregation's Yahoo groups mailing list. Over the next few days, some twenty suggestions came his way, along with several other messages begging him to share the results of his inquiry. So, he posted the answers he'd received on the mailing list, sorted by town.

Each response was quite personal. The members of the congregation identified themselves, suggested a particular dentist, and added comments motivating their recommendations. One congregant wrote, "I get the impression from our discussions of my tooth problems that he's an excellent and compassionate dentist, not to mention a better communicator than most." Another wrote, "I love my dentist. I've gone to her for over 15 years—there aren't many things I have done for 15 years in my life!"

By combining the motivations given for a particular dentist with the level of trust they had in the member of the congregation offering the recommendation, everyone on the mailing list could do personal coolhunting for a dentist. This is coolhunting on a personal level, and choosing the trendsetters they trusted most—their friends in their congregation.

In the dentist example, the simple online tool was a basic website and e-mail. The Web, though, offers many more tools for coolhunting.

Do-It-Yourself Coolhunting in the Blogosphere

Over the last few years, the World Wide Web has seen a proliferation of blogs. Under the label of "Web 2.0," some pundits even speak of the buildup of a second e-business bubble, mostly because of the emergence of do-it-yourself technologies on the Web. These include *wikis*, which are websites or other online resources where users can add and edit content collectively. In addition, there is *podcasting*—a method of publishing files to the Internet that allows users to subscribe to a feed and receive new files automatically. Then there are *blogs*.

The word "weblog" was coined in 1997; the term "blog" followed in 1999. Blogs are websites that often take the form of online diaries, periodically updated. Simple form-based editing makes it easy for blog authors—called "bloggers"—to post new entries, especially as compared with traditional websites. Bloggers blog about everything imaginable, ranging from geeky news on Slashdot.org to introducing weird gizmos on boingboing.net to the daily loves and other life exploits of single New Yorkers (a category that "boasts" dozens of blogs). What makes blogs different from online forums, mailing lists, and other similar types of online communication is that only the blog author or author group can post new entries. The rest of the world can do nothing more than submit a comment in response. Even group blogs such as boingboing or Slashdot are typically run by their founders functioning as benevolent dictators. They act as coolhunters, deciding which cool submissions make it to the blog front page.

As we write, blogs are undergoing the same exponential growth, as the Web did in the 1990s. According to blog search engine Technorati, the number of blogs exploded from 200,000 in early 2003 to 2 million only a year later. In April 2006, in its online "State of the Blogosphere" report, Technorati reported that it was tracking 35.3 million weblogs, "and the blogosphere we track continues to double about every 6 months. . . . The blogosphere is over 60 times bigger than it was only three years ago." The report states that 75,000 blogs are created every day—"on average, a new weblog is created every second of every day."[2] Meanwhile, blogs have become a source for late-breaking news and a formidable political force. It is Republican bloggers, for example, who are seen as largely responsible for forcing the retirement of CBS news anchorman Dan Rather after they exposed that the documents on which he based his claims about the military service record of President George W. Bush were mostly forgeries.

Blogs have their own dedicated search engines and so-called meta directories that rank their popularity. Technorati is the best-known, but there are many others, such as Feedster and Blogdigger. Technorati works like Google: Users enter a search string, but the results returned include only blogs. Technorati also provides a popularity ranking for all the blogs it indexes. This ranking is hugely important for bloggers, because most of them are not paid to blog. Their compensation comes in the form of "egoboosting" units, just like Open Source software developers. If you are like most bloggers, the position of your blog within the blogosphere matters a lot to you, and many bloggers are willing to do whatever it takes to move up in the rankings.

The tendency of bloggers to "game the system" and get their posts noticed is a godsend for coolhunters. Why? Because it's all about who links to you or to your blog. That is a simple idea pioneered by Google, based on the insight that somebody is measured not by whom she knows but by who knows her. If Peter sends an e-mail to Bill Gates, that's nothing special; Bill Gates probably gets thousands of e-mails from strangers. But if Bill Gates answers Peter's e-mail within the next five minutes, that would make Peter truly prominent. This translates into the blogosphere like this: If Scott is just your run-of-the-mill blogger and links to a famous blog such as boingboing or Slashdot, it does nothing to make him special. But if boingboing or Slashdot link back to Scott, that makes him and his blog truly outstanding. Typically, then, bloggers try to get noticed

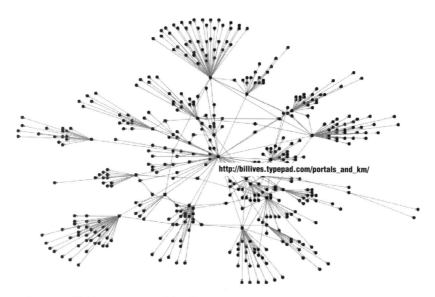

FIGURE 7–1. Linking structure of the "Portals and KM" blog. (Picture produced with TeCFlow.)

and have the top blogs place on their pages links back to their own blogs. This linking behavior can be analyzed by blog search engines and blog meme trackers (explained below) to discover new trends and trendsetters in the blogosphere.

Figure 7–1 illustrates that "you are who links to you," using as an example the "Portals and KM"[3] blog written by Peter's friend Bill Ives. Bill's blog is in the center, but he very much wants to know what other blogs link to his blog. The more links the blogs linking to his blog have, the higher position Bill's blog attains in the blogosphere. Bill is an up-and-coming blogger: Although not yet in the top 1000 blogs as ranked by Technorati, his is one of the leading blogs discussing knowledge management topics. Figure 7–1 shows that his galaxy structure is building up, with the blogs linking to his blog starting to exhibit cross-links.

This cross-linkage structure is now used by websites that mine blogs to discover new trends—such as memeorandum[4] and digg.[5] These sites are detecting memes, looking to discover new trends by continuously analyzing the blogosphere. Richard Dawkins, who coined the word "meme" in 1976, defines it as "a unit of cultural transmission, or a unit of imitation." He offers several examples: "tunes, ideas, catch-phrases, clothes fashions, ways of making pots or of building arches." Dawkins compares the transfer of memes to genes:

> Just as genes propagate themselves in the gene pool by leaping from body to body via sperms or eggs, so memes propagate themselves in the meme pool by leaping from brain to brain via a process which, in the broad sense, can be called imitation.[6]

How do memeorandum and digg work? They gauge the popularity of new posts, but they do so using different measurements. Some Web 2.0 writers draw a distinction between "meme trackers" like memeorandum, which rank posts automatically based on link structures, and "meme diggers" such as digg or del.icio.us, which let users do the meme tagging and ranking. Blogging pioneer Dave Winer, author of Scripting News[7] (one of the first weblogs, and begun in 1997) complains that memeorandum has led to "one blogger trying to top another for the most vacuous post."[8] For coolhunters, however, the meme detection services provide a great way to see who and what is cool in the blogosphere.

Initially, blogs were something used only by technophiles, and it is no accident that the first blog to attract large numbers of users was Slashdot—still the most popular online hangout for geeks and widely considered to be among the prime sites on the Web to learn about new tech trends. With the blogosphere becoming more and more mainstream, blogs now also talk about trends and trendsetters in the nontech world. Check out memeorandum's sister site WeSmirch.com, a self-described "automatic dirt digger" that will tell you all the latest blogging gossip about celebrities and wannabes. In the future, we expect to see websites coolhunting the blogosphere for just about any topic you can imagine.

Internet technology is not only making traditional news media obsolete for trend detection, but it also helps to discover interaction patterns directly between potential trendsetters. Today's ubiquitous communication technologies, such as Radio Frequency Identification (RFID), Bluetooth, and Wi-Fi, are additional coolhunting tools that make it possible to track people and their interactions with others, creating transparency and facilitating the discovery of trends and trendsetters. RFID works by storing and remotely retrieving data through devices known as tags or transponders. Most readers will be familiar with the use by scientists of small chips implanted in certain animals to study their migration patterns. Those are RFID tags. Transponders are, for example, the devices drivers use in their cars that allow them to travel through turnpike toll booths and have the toll charge billed automatically to an established account.

Tracking Physical Interactions in Social Networks

Dr. Nathan Eagle, while a doctoral student at the Massachusetts Institute of Technology's Media Lab, used another method of tracking location, based on smart mobile phones that employ the Bluetooth communication protocol. Bluetooth is an open standard, wireless technology that creates Personal Area Networks (PANs), allowing short-range transmission of digital voice and data among nearby mobile and desktop devices.

REALITY MINING

Nathan's experiment—he calls it "reality mining"[9]—gives cool-hunters a unique opportunity to discover trends and trendsetters by tracking physical movements. One hundred students and staff members who agreed to share their location information with Nathan were given free location-aware mobile phones. Over the course of nearly a year, Nathan tracked all their movements and communication activities, logging some 350,000 hours of data. Among other things, this allowed him to distinguish between *high-entropy individuals*—those who lead a very active life, move around all the time, and meet frequently with their student colleagues—and *low-entropy individuals*. How could Nathan make that distinction? He knew that two active mobile phone-carrying students were meeting when the two mobile phones stayed close to each other for longer periods of time. He also tracked their rates of moving around from one place to the next, and their frequency of engaging into new social contacts in places like discos, restaurants, and bars. Another piece of entropy information was how actively they used their mobile phones to communicate with one another. Combining these different tidbits of social information enabled Nathan to come up with distinctive entropy patterns for different people.

What Nathan discovered was that the MIT Media Lab staff was the least entropic, and freshmen students the most entropic. He also discovered that the students at the MIT Sloan School of Management were significantly less entropic than were their peers at the Media Lab. Further analysis of the communication patterns revealed that each person had a characteristic, highly individualistic communication fingerprint. Nathan correlated his findings with background information collected from his study subjects by more conventional means, such as questionnaires asking them with whom they were friends. Nathan was then able to confirm whether two people were friends, based on their proximity patterns. He found, for example, that people reported as friends at the Media Lab spent, on average, 12 minutes together during a workday, compared with the 2.9 minutes non-friends spent together.

Nathan's system can also be used to construct a life log of a person, reminding her precisely where she was at any given time in her past. The system can answer all sorts of questions: "Where did I go after leaving Peter's house last week?" or "When was the last time I had lunch with Scott?" But even cooler, Nathan can use a life log to make predictions, particularly by combining it with the life logs of other people. The system could also answer these kinds of questions: "How likely will it be that I will be meeting Mike in the next hour?" or "Will I be working in the office next weekend?" And the accuracy rate for Nathan was 85 percent. Coolhunting becomes ubiquitous!

After the experiment, Nathan discussed possible commercial uses of his system. One large networking company was "interested in handing out phones to its employees to learn how its organization really works, compared with how the company's organizational chart says it works."[10] It sounds to us like a powerful tool for helping to uncover Collaborative Innovation Networks—but, of course, must be used ethically, with privacy considerations clearly respected.

NTAGS

Dr. Rick Borovoy, also a former MIT graduate student, tried an experiment using "smart badges," a type of RFID device pioneered by the Media Lab. They track the location and physical proximity of people in an organization, thereby revealing social networks with the potential to innovate and create cool trends. Borovoy has turned his research into a startup company making social networking more ubiquitous.

Rick Borovoy's "nTags" are active badges that recognize when another wearer of an active badge gets close. Wearers of nTags can enter into a database a personal profile that describes themselves and their personal interests. If another wearer of an nTag with similar interests gets close, the nTag can initiate appropriate action, such as blinking.

At a research meeting of the worldwide food company MasterFoods, attended by hundreds of researchers who had never before met, the nTag was used as an icebreaker. Attendees could tell, from the nTag, when someone with similar interests came near. MasterFood also set up a large electronic billboard that illustrated to attendees how their personal network was growing over time. At the beginning of the event, every person was an isolated dot. At the end of the day, the billboard showed one connected community.

At a conference attended by 1,300 people, nTags were also used as icebreakers. Conference attendees were given the opportunity to enter their profiles on a Web page—participation was 100 percent—and whenever they got close to another nTag, they would learn interesting tidbits about the other person. These tidbits about their conversation partners were sent from the Web database to their nTags. Conference attendees could also use their nTags to give immediate feedback to the presenters at the end of each conference session. The conference organizers were also able to find, immediately, the great "connectors" among attendees—people who were speaking to large numbers of other people.

Just as with Nathan Eagle's mobile phones, Rick Borovoy's nTags allow for predicting the future. Conference organizers were able to learn about the preferences of 1,300 people, as well as identify the people who functioned as connectors and trendsetters. The organizers knew which people had been active participants and had given useful feedback about the current or future conferences. The organizers also knew about the networking behavior of each attendee. Combining these two pieces of information revealed the trendsetters to conference organizers: people who were great networkers and who also contributed new ideas.

Participants could enter their ideas at any time during the conference. The organizers gathered the ideas about the current and future conferences and presented them to the participants, who could then vote on them using their nTags. This way, conference attendees could immediately influence the progress of the conference and future developments. It is a perfect example of the conference organizers giving power away: participants could shape future conferences themselves—and, in a sense, predict the future of these conferences—leading to more attractive and better attended conferences.

WIRELESS SENSORS

Mark Feldmeier, a graduate student at the MIT Media Lab, along with Professor Joe Paradiso, have also been building some very simple—and very cool—"featherweight" wireless sensors. While their system was designed for interactive entertainment, they see possibilities for using it to monitor the integrity of shipping packages or create "intelligent" homes. Josha Randall, a former MIT undergraduate in electrical engineering and computer science and lighting designer for many MIT stage productions, figured out how to use it as a lighting controller that would allow large groups to interact directly with the lighting system.[11] For now, the sensors are low-cost (using a simple coin cell battery and minimal circuitry keeps them under $1.00 each when fabricated in large quantities), wireless, and wearable, and they make it possible for large groups of people—up to hundreds of thousands—to participate simultaneously in an activity. They tried the system out at several MIT dances. Everyone was given a sensor encapsulated in a lucite glow tube for easy handling (not to mention that kids—even college kids—like glowing tubes, just like the ones that are so common among trick-or-treaters on Halloween). The sensors send data that reflects the activity and state of the participants dancing to rhythmic and nonrhythmic music. In the case of music with a clear rhythm, the synchronization of the swarm to a definite tempo can be measured, corresponding to the beats-per-minute of the music being played. And, "if one observes the activity and tempo plots across an hour of dance (with about 20 participants), structure is clearly seen as dancers go through cycles of increased/decreased activity and push the tempo higher when the generated tempo is set to be above the measured tempo."[12] The data can drive changes in the music—for instance, it might grow more complex and "wilder" as people dance more.

The system distinguishes between different families of sensors, such as those that might be attached to the hands or feet, but does not independently identify each person who has a sensor. The sensors have been designed for only a very slight probability of overlap, even when people are trying to synchronize their activity. It's all about extracting swarm statistics from "ensemble behavior." And it bodes well for coolhunting the trends swarms create.

Finding Learning Trends and Making Education Cooler

Not all trends are related to ideas and products, and not all trends—which are directions demonstrated through observation of data and/or indicators over time—are positive. Sometimes, the direction found through observation or measurement can be negative, but it can still be very cool to uncover even a negative trend, especially when it comes with the power to turn it positive. Consider, for instance, a classroom.

Students at some 300 universities in the United States are using handheld, infrared transmitters in their classrooms to respond to teachers' questions during lectures. The transmitters closely resemble television remotes. The value of this application of simple radio frequency technology—what makes it so cool—is that it allows for a real-time feedback loop between student and teacher about whether the subject matter is comprehensible, instead of waiting to an end-of-term test to find out that the lecture went right over everyone's head.

Here's how it works at Duke University in Durham, North Carolina. A professor poses, say, a multiple-choice question and the students transmit their responses, captured by small receivers installed around the classroom. When polling ends, a chart shows the class the percentage of students favoring each answer. What's especially cool is that this affords the professor a chance to gauge the overall comprehension level and make adjustments right then and there.

"When I just ask students if everybody understands something, there's not a sound out of 75 students," explains William McNairy, a Duke University lecturer in physics. "But after class, five students ask me to go over something again. For them, it's OK, but for the others, it's too late. If the classroom response shows 70 percent of the class gets something right, I feel somewhat confident that they understand it. If it's 20 percent, I can spend more time on the topic."[13] Other teachers at schools across the country—including high schools and middle schools—report that students who might otherwise never raise their hands and admit to being confused or not understanding something are much more likely to speak when the entire group is prompted by the teacher, using the results from this technology.

The InterWrite "clickers"—as even the manufacturer, GTCO CalComp, calls them—can also be used for in-class quizzes, which can be graded immediately. A student at Coeur d'Alene High School in Idaho told the Associated Press that "instantaneous feedback was a huge advantage" in her third-year Spanish class. Her teacher believes the clickers enhance the lessons and "noticed about a 15 to 20 percent increase in [student's] oral grades and their quiz grades." He no longer needs to "guess whether kids know [the subject matter] to the best of their ability"—he can "actually see it." Other teachers, too, report that they believe students learn more using the remotes. An Ohio State University professor of agricultural economics says that a class he taught using the technology "was possibly the best performing class I've had in the five years I've been teaching it. . . . They understood the material well and the students really like it."[14] Teachers are giving away power to the students, who get new chances to shape and influence the educational process. Rather than sitting in the classroom as passive listeners, students can become trendsetters. And the coolest thing is that it's not just for the most extroverted and outspoken students, but for the entire swarm!

The Interwriter "clickers" are mostly used for single-classroom teaching. But the Internet also enables synchronous and asynchronous collaboration between trendsetters spread out at multiple locations. In a course on swarm creativity Peter taught in Fall 2005, students at the University of Cologne, Germany, and Helsinki University of Technology in Finland formed virtual project teams, coolhunting for trends and trendsetters as distributed COINs. The course was taught partly from the Massachusetts Institute of Technology, thus combining three locations simultaneously. The course taught us invaluable lessons for virtual collaboration among coolhunters and coolfarmers.

Some Lessons for Virtual Collaboration

The student groups in this course faced several challenges during their virtual collaboration. The students in Germany had not met the students in Finland in person, or vice versa, and so they had little knowledge of each other and of working styles. This caused some confusion. It was challenging to get a real sense of "teamwork."

The difficulties were greatest in the early going. Student teams found it quite hard to set up efficient work processes, so it took some time. Groups in which one team member simply took the lead and just "did it" got a head start.

In Figure 7–2, you see the virtual classroom created by video-conferencing the participants together in Helsinki, Cologne, and Cambridge. This setting was used to create the feeling of a virtual team and nurture the emergence of COINs. Each classroom had two video projectors, and a camera. On one video projection screen (the picture on the left), the remote classrooms were shown simultaneously. On a second projector, the course agenda was shown concurrently in Cambridge, Cologne, and Helsinki (the top-right picture). This setting permitted all members of the course to address each other directly and to get to know the remote members of each team "personally."

The student teams were formed during a videoconference session: the students joined together in groups based on their interest

FIGURE 7–2. Snapshots from teaching the course through videoconferencing.

in suggested topics. The only rule was that all the groups should have students from both countries. If a group had at least two students from the same country, this led to the formation of co-located subgroups that communicated at least partly through means other than e-mail, such as phone or face-to-face. This excluded team members not co-located from some communication. For groups having only a sub-group of a single student in the other country, this was especially problematic. The isolated student found it difficult to follow activities in the other country.

Even though e-mail was the main communication medium, some groups started to use Skype's chat and voice capabilities, or used other chat programs—particularly for coordinating the work and making decisions. The synchronous communication was regarded as very efficient, but the problem was to find meeting times suitable to all group members. This problem often led to Skype or chat sessions between only two members at a time.

E-mail communication functioned quite well, but because it is relatively slow and not very interactive it was regarded as a less-efficient communication medium than was Skype or chat for intensive collaboration. Decision making was particularly difficult via e-mail. Moreover, the asynchronicity of e-mail communication created uncertainty when others did not know how to interpret the silence of the nonresponding team member. Interpreting sent e-mail messages was also not always easy. While English was the language used in the course, translating from "Finnish" English to "German" English and vice versa created a lot of room for interpretation.

Although there was active communication within the teams, communication across groups was very limited and took place mainly during class videoconference sessions. This was unfortunate; communication across groups would have been beneficial, for example, in overcoming obstacles using software tools such as the ones described in this and the next chapter. Setting up a discussion forum for technical communication problems would also have helped. Questions to the teachers could have been directed to this forum, allowing everybody to follow and participate in these discussions.

To exclude local communication hidden from nonlocal team members, various solutions can be pursued. The most radical solution is to only allow one team member from each location and organize project teams across several sites. This will enforce that all communication across the different sites will be electronic—such as e-mail, chat, or Skype—and thus easier to record and easier for other team members to follow. The learning from this course on coolhunting and coolfarming will be discussed in greater detail in Chapter 10.

Nascent trends and trendsetters, working together in swarm creativity, can also be discovered automatically. In Chapter 8, we'll see this in action, as pictures of social networks are generated by mining communication logs and archives.

8

Coolhunting by Automated Social Network Analysis

Social structure becomes actually visible in an anthill; the movements and contacts one sees are not random but patterned. We should also be able to see structure in the life of an American community if we had a sufficiently remote vantage point, a point from which persons would appear to be small moving dots....We should see that these dots do not randomly approach one another, that some are usually together, some meet often, some never ....If one could get far enough away from it, human life would become pure pattern.

—Roger Brown, social network theorist[1]

IN CHAPTER 1, we introduced the basic principles of social network analysis. Here we introduce a software tool and, later in the chapter, demonstrate how those principles can be applied to discover both trends and trendsetter in an automated way by mining communication archives.

Discovering Trends by Mining Communication Archives

The goal of mining communication archives is to discover both obvious and hidden relationships among people. Relationships can range from one person giving advice to another or people working together on the same project, to one person reporting to another in a boss-subordinate relationship or even friendship networks.

The more messages two people exchange, the stronger is their relationship. Messages can be anything recorded by an electronic archive, including e-mails, phone calls, online chat sessions, or links embedded into a blog. As Dr. David Clark, one of the original inventors of the internet, observed:

> It is not proper to think of networks as connecting computers. Rather, they connect people using computers to mediate. The great success of the Internet is not technical, but in human impact. Electronic mail may not be a wonderful advance in Computer Science, but it is a whole new way for people to communicate.[2]

In our work, we have been using a social network analysis and visualization software tool called *TeCFlow*, created by Peter and his student Yan Zhao. TeCFlow creates interactive, dynamic movies of relationships by analyzing and visualizing the evolution of a social network over time and providing a snapshot of the social network at any given point. It analyzes relationships among people, among organizations, among keywords, and among websites and blogs. It also visualizes and analyzes the evolution of changes in the linking networks of these groups, identifying the most relevant, central, and influential people and the content of their discussion at any given time. When you watch theses snapshots combined into a movie, you can see who is acting as an influencer, gatekeeper, leader, or laggard, as well as observe any changes in these roles.

TeCFlow also analyzes and visualizes the evolution of semantic networks and concept maps over time. A *semantic network* is a system for

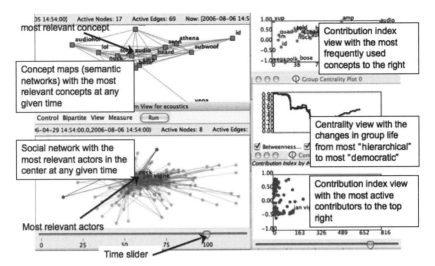

FIGURE 8–1. A snapshot of an online community analyzed over time, using TeCFlow.

capturing, storing, and transferring information, and is often used as a form of knowledge representation. The network is depicted as a directed graph consisting of vertices that represent concepts and edges that represent semantic relations among the concepts. A *concept map* is a diagram that makes visual the relationship among concepts, which are shown as nodes or cells. The links among concepts are labeled and direction is denoted with an arrow in a downward-branching hierarchical structure. The relationship among concepts is articulated in linking phrases such as "gives rise to" or "results in" or "is required by" or "contributes to"—among others.

Figure 8–1 is a snapshot of an online community analyzed over time, using the TeCFlow tool.

The centrality view at the middle right of Figure 8-1 shows how centrality in a social network changes over time. In a highly centralized network, one person dominates the network, sitting as a hub in the center of the network—think of a strict hierarchy with a boss in control of communication and decision making. In a low-centrality network, everyone interacts with many other people across the network—think of an egalitarian team where each person communicates directly with everyone else without asking the boss for permission.

The contribution index (on the right in Figure 8-1, showing each person as a dot) measures the activity of people as senders and receivers of messages within a group. The basic idea is that the more someone is a sender of messages, the more she contributes to the community. To test this assumption, though, the number of messages she receives is also factored in; this accounts for the person who might "spam" the community with messages just to be measured as the most active contributor. If a heavy sender also receives many messages, she must truly play an important role within her community. The more active contributors are, the more to the right they will be shown; the more active senders are, the higher they will be in the picture. The most active senders, who coordinate a community, are shown in the upper-right corner of the contribution index view.

The analysis shows synchronized changes in central positions of social actors and core concepts and predicts future linking behavior based on the past communication behavior of social actors. In addition, TeCFlow visually identifies and measures the most relevant,

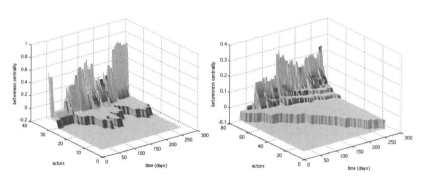

FIGURE 8–2. *Temporal social surfaces of a COIN (left) and group with shared interests (right).*

central, and influential people and concepts in the social and semantic networks. Finally, it identifies and visually analyzes communication patterns of the most creative and performing teams by computing "temporal social surfaces"—a visual instrument Peter developed to distinguish communication patterns in different types of teams.

The picture on the left of Figure 8–2 shows the temporal social surface of a COIN comprising 40 people ("actors") over a period of 300 days. The "height" of the surface shows how central an actor is at any given time. Most COIN members are inactive at any given time, but it's easy to identify individual activity, as well as that of large parts of the group, as "elevated planes" and "peaks" in the surface.

There are five phases in this COIN's lifecycle. After initial kick-off by a few central actors, a larger group of about ten people communicates with low centrality. This is followed by a first period during which collaboration by about five central members with about twenty peripheral people peaks. In the next phase, total participation decreases, as shown by the decrease in the width of the centrality "hills". The five original members communicate with low centrality, which means that everyone talks to everyone else. In the final phase, there are two or three highly central members communicating with about twenty peripheral participants.

The picture on the right of Figure 8–2 shows a completely different temporal social surface: the social network of eighty members of a church. We can see four levels of membership, illustrated by three "plateaus." The large majority, on the first plateau, are passive members who have very low centrality—that is, they switch over time from being not involved at all to being passive recipients of messages when they join the church. There is a slowly growing group of increasingly central people on the three levels of active membership. On the second plateau, we find a group of three to five people of modest centrality. Then there is another small group of constant size. Finally, there is a growing group of three to ten most-active members of the community who are very central (most likely the minister and his assistants).

In the following five examples, we show how automated social network analysis can be a great coolhunting tool. Mining communication archives such as a phone log, an online forum, a Wiki, or an e-mail archive, you can visually identify the leaders, influencers, and gatekeepers of each community by drawing the social network with a tool such as TeCFlow. And by adding the *content* of communication to the analytic mix, you can identify the trends trendsetters are talking about.

1. Identifying Trendsetters in a Social Network: Wikinews

Wikinews is an outgrowth of Wikipedia, the free online encyclopedia open to contributions and editing by anyone. The original goal of Wikinews was to be for news what Wikipedia is for encyclopedias—the ultimate source of information maintained through swarm creativity. Wikinews creators originally hoped that news would be uploaded by volunteer reporters whenever they would stumble upon something newsworthy. They expected that among the witnesses of a newsworthy event there would always be enough amateur journalists to cover the event for Wikinews. Let's see whether the original assumption of the Wikinews creators was true.

As a class project, a team of Peter's students (Sebastian Schiefer and Lutz Tegethoff at the University of Cologne, and Ilkka Lyytinen at the Helsinki University of Technology) used automated social network analysis to analyze the profile of the Wikinews contributors. Sebastian, Lutz, and Ilkka set out to discover the trendsetters among the Wikinews contributors, and also to see whether they could find the most talked about news items within the news they

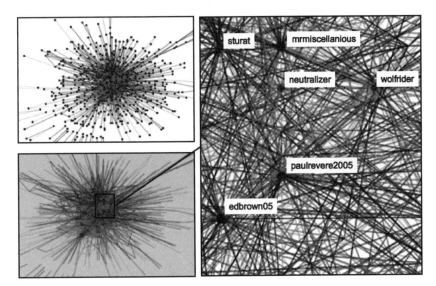

FIGURE 8–3. Leaders among the Wikinews contributors.

were analyzing. Using social networking analysis, they modeled coauthorship of news posts as social relationships, in particular between the creator of an article and the subsequent editors of the same article. They based their analysis on data they gathered from articles posted between November 2004 and November 2005, comprising the Wikinews project's first year of communication activity.

In their analysis, the students came up with some interesting findings. Figure 8–3 identifies the most central people among the volunteer journalists. They found that the most central people in the network of Wikinews contributors were those who held administrative rights. The administrators are the "leaders" of the Wikinews community, deciding whether certain news items need to be protected from malicious users. This means that every change made to a "write-protected" news entry needs to be approved by an administrator. Administrators also decide on expelling rogue users—a user who, for example, continues to make edits with content that violate the standards of Wikinews.

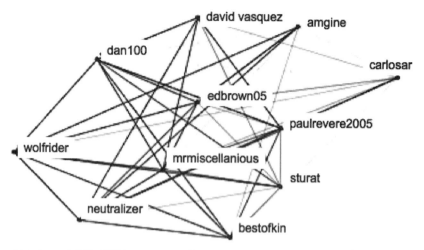

FIGURE 8–4. COIN of Wikinews core editors.

As Figure 8–3 shows, administrators are in the most central positions—just as the Wikinews community expected would be the case for those responsible for coordinating other users. This tells us that the Wikinews swarm chooses its leaders well.

The students then looked at how the roles of the most central contributors changed. They were able to identify, for example, "quality control" people who played a very central role, but who rarely submitted original news items. Rather, these people edited other people's contributions to get them to a higher level of quality. Their communication structure, in which everyone had direct contact with everyone else, indicates working as a Collaborative Innovation Network, swarming together to clean up each others' and other people's posts (see Figure 8–4).

Combining social network analysis and content analysis, the student researchers also tried to find the subject matter experts—journalists who were covering a certain topic or a geographic region—hoping to discover the first reporters to write about a hot new story. This proved impossible, with one exception. They found a thread of stories covering the huge tsunami that devastated the Indian Ocean coastline on December 26, 2004.

The tsunami is one of the deadliest disasters of modern times; the death toll came to well more than 200,000 people, counting the missing who could not be accounted for. The victims were not only the mostly poor, indigenous residents of remote areas of Thailand, Sri Lanka, Indonesia, India, and seven other affected countries, but also thousands of tourists from Western countries on Christmas holiday. Among the tourists who survived were plenty of amateur journalists to cover the story for Wikinews.

How could the students tell that the tsunami was being covered by a small group of volunteers reporting first-hand? They were able to find the volunteer reporter who submitted the original stories, which were then edited by other tourists who were also Wikinews volunteer reporters. The top left window of Figure 8–5 illustrates the social network of all Wikinews contributors during the tsunami

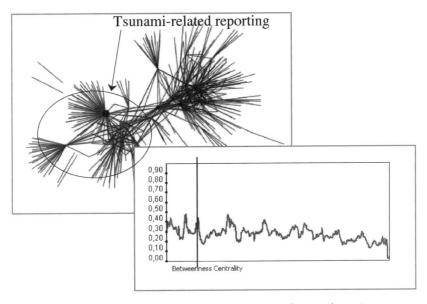

FIGURE 8–5. *Reporters and betweenness centrality curve of tsunami events.*

period. The left cluster with the one central coordinator (the largest dot) shows the main editor embedded in a network of other tsunami reporters. The cluster at right is the network of all the other reporters covering news not about the tsunami.

The curve in the lower window shows the changes in the social network structure of the Wikinews contributors over time. The larger the values on the curve are, the more the social network is dominated by one or a few people. We can clearly identify the spike in betweenness centrality,[3] marked by the vertical line, when the coordinator of the Wikinews volunteers covering the tsunami takes over and centralizes communication.

Figure 8–6 shows the complete term network during coverage of the tsunami. It contains the semantic network of the most important terms in all the messages posted, including terms used in stories unrelated to the tsunami. Again, we notice a clear clustering of the tsunami-related terms in the lower left of the picture.

Reporting of the tsunami-related event was the only one, however, where the students could clearly identify a group of "witness

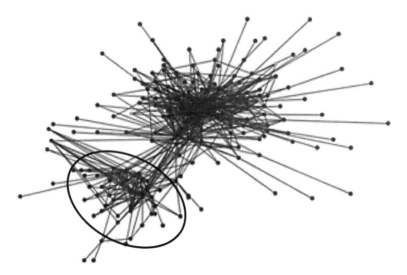

FIGURE 8–6. Terms of tsunami event.

reporters" covering an incident for Wikinews they had experienced themselves. They came to this conclusion by studying coauthor networks of all the stories covered in the first year of operation. While there are other "original" articles, these are usually just condensations of other news stories—an indication that the Wikinews goal of having "witness reporters" contribute genuinely original, late-breaking news had not yet been achieved.[4] The students looked at other major news stories, trying to find contributors uploading news they personally witnessed. What they found is that in most cases Wikinews contributors simply spread news they had found through other sources. Thanks to automated social network analysis, the student team was able to identify the one news story that was covered directly by the trendsetting journalists: the tsunami.

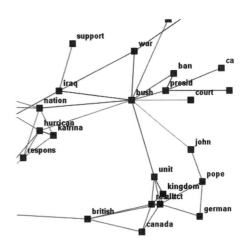

FIGURE 8–7. Most central terms in Wikinews' semantic network of terms. (Note: In a process called "stemming," the software tool cuts off the ends of words.)

By doing a social network-based content analysis of posted messages, the students were able to create an overview of the most important events over the one-year span presented in correct chronological order. Figure 8–7 shows one snapshot of the movie of the most central terms that TeCFlow generates. Watching the entire movie, one can recognize the tsunami catastrophe, the election of a new pope, the British elections, the terrorist attacks on the London subway, Hurricane Katrina, and the earthquake in Pakistan. The term "Bush" was quite central during the whole time and was strongly connected to the term "Iraq"—also a central term and almost constantly connected to the term "war."

Automated social network analysis could be used for both coolhunting and coolfarming at Wikinews. Coolhunting new trends would permit Wikinews readers to find the "coolest" news both as it first arises and retrospectively. As a coolfarming tool, it would allow for monitoring the development of the contributor community and measuring a user's importance as a news editor—thus finding the trendsetters among the contributors. This information could be used to enhance collaboration. The community could, for example, find the most trusted and central members. If those are not yet administrators, they could be offered this status.

Remember the four principles of coolfarming we articulated in Chapter 5. Wikinews already delegates authorship to its readers— it *gives power away*. By presenting news stories, Wikinews *seeds the community with ideas*; the community then takes up these stories and edits them. Wikinews also *mandates intrinsic motivation*—by applying dynamic social network analysis, the Wikinews community knows who are the most dedicated editors. The fourth principle of coolfarming includes the search for new trendsetters, which is what this student team did when they found the original contributor and later coordinator of the tsunami story. While the students' work was "only" for a university term paper, the same coolfarming principles could be applied by the Wikinews community.

As the example in Chapter 1 of Continental's frequent flyers shows, the Web offers a seemingly limitless supply of online communities like Wikinews to study. Typically, their members are not only trendsetters and early adopters of emerging technologies, but they are also very outspoken in their opinions. These online communities, therefore, provide an excellent coolhunting ground—as we see in the next example.

2. Coolhunting New Product Trends in an Online Forum: eCoustics

Using the same automated social networking analysis approach as their colleagues who studied Wikinews, another team of Peter's students (Di Zhu, Jing Jing, and Manta Jääskeläinen from Helsinki University of Technology, and Paul Willems from the University of Cologne) analyzed the eCoustics forum, an online discussion of the latest trends in loudspeakers.[5] Paul, Manta, Di, and Jing collected a half-year's worth of discussions about loudspeakers, a total of 16,000 posts submitted by 1,100 contributors. They constructed social relationships between members by looking at who responded to whom, and who participated with which other members in the same thread. The most connected member, who goes by the pseudonym of "Jan Vigne," has more than 1,000 links. "Jan Vigne," though, is not the most active poster; that distinction goes to "Edster922."

Figure 8–8 illustrates the full social network created by all the posts over this six-month period.

Not much can be seen in Figure 8–8. Looking at the network in smaller time slices is much more insightful. Figures 8–9 to 8–11

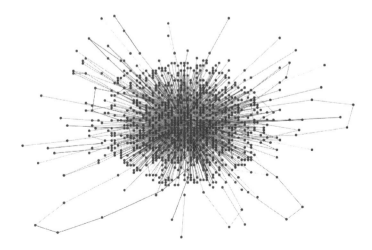

FIGURE 8–8. Full social network of the eCoustics forum over a six-months period.

show three snapshots of a movie of the social network, illustrating how the online community is growing.

At the beginning of April (Figure 8–9), the forum has a small number of members communicating in diversely distributed clusters. There is little group connection; each member is only connected to a few other members, and there is no discernible cluster of people recognizable in the core.

At the end of April, though, clusters are connected and merged (Figure 8–10). The online community begins to form a small core of six users, linked to a large peripheral group.

Through the end of October, the core grows to include about fifteen users (Figure 8–11). Some of them are new and highly active members; others are old members who lost their central position and move to the periphery of the network. This means that they are no longer active members of the community anymore, but have become occasional posters. The most active members are always shown in the core.

Figure 8–12 shows the same network, but includes now only the most active participants. There is a group of key contributors who are the most active users and form a core network. Most of the others among the 1,100 users of eCoustics are visitors, asking questions and receiving answers from these active users in the core group. The active fifteen users assume the central position, connecting many other people. The snapshots in Figure 8–12 show these trendsetters; the same people are colored with identical colors across the different months. The larger the dot representing a person is, the more central a role that person plays.

As we already saw in Figures 8–9, 8–10, and 8–11, there was a huge increase in new members; the peak growth time was from April to July. The summer months saw the most activity in the forum. This was true for both the absolute number of posts as well as for

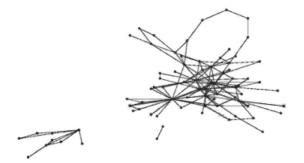

FIGURE 8–9. eCoustics forum at the beginning of April.

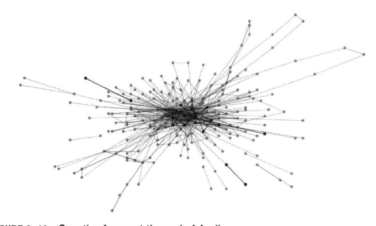

FIGURE 8–10. eCoustics forum at the end of April.

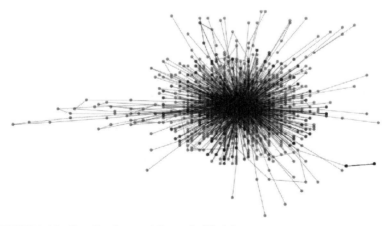

FIGURE 8–11. eCoustics forum at the end of October.

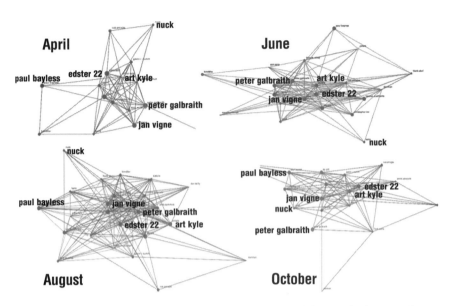

FIGURE 8–12. *Monthly snapshots of eCoustics forum social network of most active members.*

the number of users participating in the forum. The most popular thread was in July, on the topic "Bookshelfs - $400 a pair - too many choices! - OVERWHELMED!" It generated 158 posts. In August, another topic—"The future of speakers"—generated 154 posts. Also in August, there were 109 posts on the topic: "Ring of the Lings, Part 3: Quinn's turn."

The student research team analyzed these posts, tracking their communication pattern through time. They investigated the threads in which certain combinations of words appeared and analyzed the interaction between users to track the propagation of different opinions on issues such as the "best bookshelves for less than $400," or "the future of speakers." They were able to find the trendsetters and the creative people acting as gatekeepers, who introduced new ideas about a subject that then spawned new subthreads. The students did this by searching for textual patterns that reappeared in different threads. They were also able to identify non-obvious connections between seemingly unrelated topics, based on social links between the posters.

The eCoustics example illustrates how automated social network analysis can be used to discover new trends among the "best bookshelves for less than $400" not simply by counting how many mentions there are of a particular product, but by analyzing the contents of the online forum and thus showing *how* the discussion among participants unfolds and in turn revealing the trend. Beyond just the trends, though, the *trendsetters*—those who influence the buying behavior of a community—can also be found. Without convening a focus group, designers and manufacturers of loudspeakers can discover what key users are thinking about their current products and coolhunt ideas trendsetters would like to see in the next generation.

The users in the eCoustics forum are the customers who care the most about the product; after all, they're going to the trouble of participating in the online forum. They function in swarm creativity: they have a shared interest in the technology and are motivated by that interest and their excitement with the product. What more could you ask for? Coolhunting eCoustics is like getting the swarm to do your market research for you. How many companies, though, are failing to take advantage of this great resource?

Our next example also shows coolhunting in action—this time with users of a product, but not through online mining.

3. Coolhunting Trendsetters Among Product Users: Mobile Phones in a High School Class

The dynamic structure of the communication network among users of a technology can help you identify who plays an influential role, who is passive, who are the technology geeks, and who might be more or less of technology-refusers or "Luddites." Uncovering the social network among the users of a technology makes it possible to coolhunt the trendsetting users and the cool trends they establish.

A large European telecommunications company wanted to define its new mobile phone product and marketing strategy and identify its target audience for advertising. The company decided to conduct an experiment in 2004 with a class of high school students, who were given free mobile phones and free calling to anyone they wanted, with no limit on time. They could even use value-added services offered on the mobile network, such as getting soccer results, accessing train schedules, or ordering cinema tickets via text messaging—all for free.

In return, the telecom company obtained the students' communication data. This included who students called and for how long, and which services they used and for how long. Of course, it also included which services they didn't use. The telecom company was after an in-depth understanding of the usage pattern of its teenage mobile phone users, and to learn about trends, trendsetters, and influencers in a peer network. With this understanding, the company would be better equipped to customize new products and services to the needs of this customer segment.

When our research group at MIT got involved,[6] the company's own researchers had already done a thorough job interviewing the students about how they were using their mobile phones. User profiles ran a wide gamut. There was the *innovator*, one of the most frequent users, who routinely sent Multimedia Message Service (MMS) movies to his peers and who was constantly requesting soccer results—at the time, the European soccer championship games were underway in Portugal. He was also experimenting with a variety of text message-based services. The *guru* racked up the highest—which, fortunately, he did not have to pay—using the mobile phone as a modem to connect his computer to the Internet while riding the train. While the *innovator* was making active use of the services, the *guru* mostly experimented with the new services, and also acted as an internal help desk and "first level mobile phone supporter" for his classmates.

Other users included the *lead users*, a group of girls and boys who became quite heavy text-messagers, employing their mobile phones to exchange Internet chat messages with their less-fortunate friends who had not received free phones and airtime. Finally, there was the *refuser*, who declared the phone unnecessary. Every other member of his immediate family already had a mobile phone, and he was under constant pressure to use the one he was given, but he stubbornly withstood this pressure during the analysis period to "remain independent." His circle of friends supported him in his decision; they, too, mostly refused to use mobile phones, not wanting to become "slaves of technology" forced to "drag around a clunky piece of equipment."

The telecom researcher working with the students had already done a first social network analysis as he sought out the social undercurrents in this group of mobile phone users. He had also done extensive interviews with all the students to understand their reasons

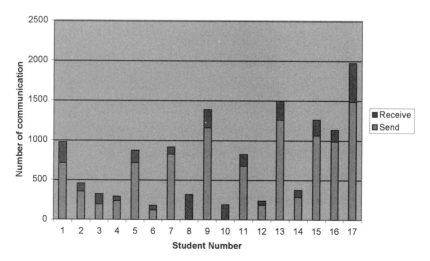

FIGURE 8–13. *Communication usage data of the seventeen mobil phone users.*

for certain usage behaviors. He then teamed up with our MIT group to gain a better understanding of the different usage patterns of the teenagers and to identify the trendsetters and lead users.

First we looked at the accumulated usage to identify the heaviest senders and receivers. We lumped together all categories of communication activities, drawing no distinction between sending or receiving a phone call or text message or contacting a value-added service. Figure 8–13 shows the complete usage of all seventeen mobile phone users over the entire period of the experiment.

Students 8 and 10—Dave and Steve—immediately stand out as *refusers*—they only used their mobile phones to receive phone calls and text messages, and never placed a call or sent a message themselves. It is interesting to note that Dave is one of the most popular receivers, getting a large amount of messages. This is already a first indication of Dave's high social status; although he refused to use the technology actively, he is very popular with his friends. Only student 17—John, the

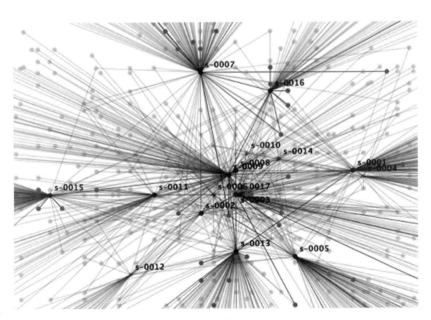

FIGURE 8–14. Full communication network with outside world.

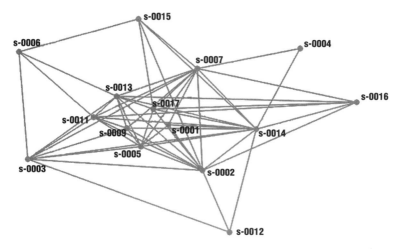

FIGURE 8–15. Class-only network.

guru—gets more messages, and remember that John became an unofficial help desk for his classmates. John is the most active in terms of sending and receiving messages.

Comparing the accumulated usage data of Figure 8–13 to the social networking picture in Figure 8–14 again reveals some interesting results. The central role of John (17) as a tech supporter of his classmates comes out clearly. Although students 5 (Mary), 7, and 15, the lead users, are quite heavy users of technology, they are not very central within the class but do communicate quite actively with outside peers. On the other hand, there are relatively low-frequency users such as students 2 and 3 (Eileen), who are nevertheless in the core of the class.

Figure 8–15 illustrates the communication within the class. All communication with people outside of the class has now been removed. John's central tech supporter role now becomes even more obvious. Other students such as 1, 5 (Mary), 9 (Sarah), 11, and 13 also are members of the inner core of the class.

It gets really interesting when we begin to compare the full communication network, including people outside the class in Figure 8–14,

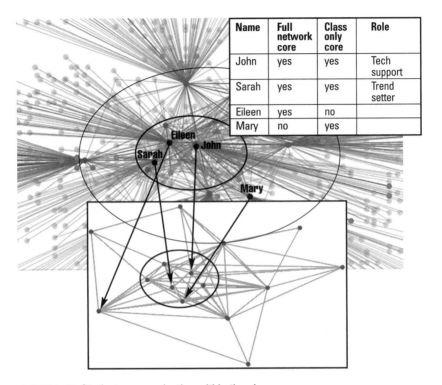

Name	Full network core	Class only core	Role
John	yes	yes	Tech support
Sarah	yes	yes	Trend setter
Eileen	yes	no	
Mary	no	yes	

FIGURE 8–16. Student communication within the class.

with the class-internal network in Figure 8–15. Figure 8–16 shows an extracted view of this comparison, pointing out the changing roles of some students.

Figure 8–17 displays a schematic view of this assessment. The three concentric light gray circles represent the full network; the two concentric dark gray circles represent the class-internal network.

Students 2 and 3 (Eileen), who were in the core of the class in the full communication picture (innermost oval on the left), become quite peripheral in the class-only communication picture (outer oval on the right). In contrast, some students (such as 7 and 12) are peripheral both in the complete network as well as in the class-internal network. Still other students who were originally peripheral in the full communication network (such as Mary, student 5) now become part of the

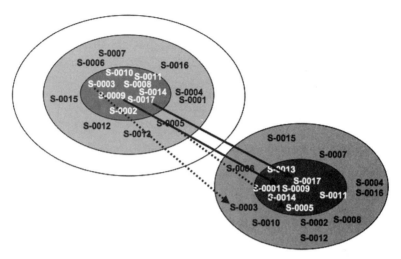

FIGURE 8–17. In the class-only network, some students become peripherals, while others move to the center.

core group in the class-internal network. Mary is a gatekeeper, linking an extensive external communication network with a large part of the class-internal communication network.

Finally, there are the students such as "innovator" student Sarah and "tech guru" student John, who are central in both the full and the class-internal communication network. From the perspective of the phone company, the students of the last two groups, the gatekeepers and the continuous members of both full and internal network, are of greatest potential interest. The telecom researcher had already verified this through student interviews that revealed the crucial innovator and tech guru roles of Sarah and John. What we are showing here is that we can do this based on the social network position of phone users by using an automated visualization tool such as TeCFlow.

In the next phase of the experiment, we zoomed in on the usage of new value-added services such as obtaining soccer results, weather forecasts, or train timetables. Figure 8–18 shows the accumulated uses of value-added services of all students. From the perspective of the phone company, these heavy users are the early adopters of new technologies. Just looking at accumulated usage, students 3, 9, and 17 stand out.

The phone company, however, has far more interest in continued usage over time, not just a one-time burst of activity. Listing all usages of the value-added services over time in Figure 8–19 identifies student 17, John, as a sporadic heavy user in the time interval between January and February 2004, but significantly scaling back in the time thereafter. Student 9, Sarah, however, continues to use value-added services heavily over the entire observation period, which marks her as a much more attractive user for the phone company. Student 3, Eileen, while a good potential customer, is probably not a big trendsetter.

In the final and most interesting part of the experiment, we also integrated the temporal dimension into our analysis. Our hypothesis was that the first user of a value-added service was the influencer—he or she would be responsible for getting other students try out the new service. Using the TeCFlow analysis tool, we created a movie showing which students (1 to 17) were using which products (P-0178 to Q-5955). Figure 8–20 illustrates the central role of *innovator* stu-

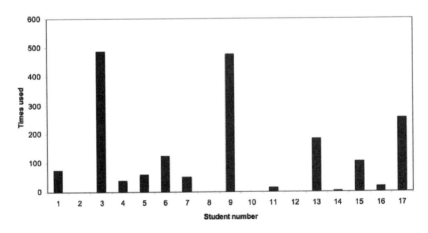

FIGURE 8–18. *New service usage pattern.*

New Services usage pattern over time

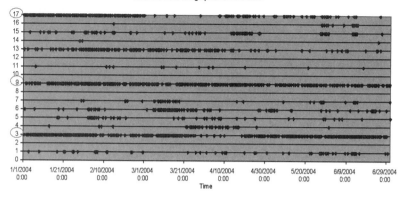

FIGURE 8–19. New service usage pattern over time.

dent 9, Sarah, who tries out an entire group of services P-0259, P-0296, P-0364, P-0345. Even better, after she uses services P-0178, P-0316, and P-0372, her colleagues 5, 1, and 7 follow her lead and also start using these new services. Sarah finds what's cool among the mobile phone services, which makes her a coolhunter. She also sets the trend for using the cool services she coolhunted, which makes her a coolfarmer. In her student swarm, Sarah is one key bee!

Tech guru student 17, John, turns out not to be very innovative in using the new services. This somewhat counters the claims he made in the interviews with the researchers of the telecom company. Figure 8–20 also easily reveals that P-0335, getting soccer results during the European soccer championship games, is the most popular service among these users.

This social network analysis-based approach helped the phone company coolhunt trends and trendsetters that would have been otherwise very difficult to spot. The company learned about high-prestige refusers such as Dave, who—although he himself never actively used his mobile phone—turned out to be central in the full-class network and the recipient of many calls and text messages. Addressing people like Dave directly, and helping him to overcome

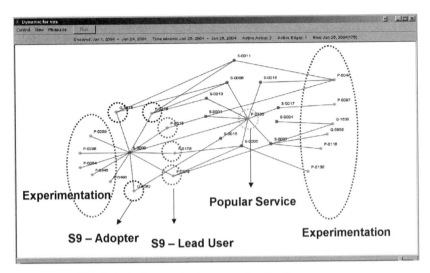

FIGURE 8–20. Which student uses which new service first?

his skepticism, would generate another highly influential trendsetter like Sarah for the telecom company. Also very interesting, the company learned about gatekeepers such as Mary, who linked an extensive external network with a central position in the class-internal network. The company also learned about influencers such as Sarah and John—they influenced their peers to use their mobile phones more heavily. Of highest interest to the company was our coolhunting discovery that trendsetters such as Sarah and influencers such as Mary can be found in an automated way just by mining the company's own communication archive.

This example speaks to the value of automated coolhunting for businesses. It stands to reason that if you can identify the trendsetters in a small peer-group community, you could generalize that they might also "represent"—that is, share characteristics with—the trendsetters in a larger population. The possibilities are almost limitless. From seventeen kids, the mobile phone company in our example could draw conclusions about hundreds of thousands of other kids who were potential users of its product. The company could conduct similar experiments with other types of peer groups and generalize from those findings, too. Once completed, the company would have a lot of intelligence to guide how best to tailor offerings to various types of mobile phone users.

The mobile phone example also suggests an excellent way of setting up focus groups for market research. Most often, people are chosen for focus groups to represent a cross-section of a larger group, based on demographics. Imagine what you might learn from a group of people all sharing the characteristics of Sarah, the innovator student in the mobile phone experiment. After she tried out the company's various services, the other students followed her lead. Sarah set the trends. A focus group of Sarahs would tell you not only what people like and why, but also that what they like is soon going to be liked by others—*many others.*

Our next automated coolhunting example illustrates how social network analysis can be used to hunt for patterns of criminal activity. Beyond that, though, it has profitable applications for general business use.

4. Discovering Suspicious Patterns of Innovation: Enron

The deceit and downright criminality of Enron's behavior—which we looked at in brief in Chapter 6—is well known and well documented. Let's dig deeper. For students of swarm creativity and coolhunting, the company's activities offer a great laboratory in which to study and compare social network patterns of trendsetters communicating and collaborating on innovations gone awry.

During the investigation of Enron's activities by the Federal Energy Regulatory Commission, the contents of the e-mail boxes of 150 Enron employees were released into the public domain. Social network researchers cleaned these up and made the data available on the Web to other researchers.[7] The Enron e-mail dataset that was used for this project consists of 517,431 messages that belong to the 150 mailboxes.

In another class project, a group of Peter's students (Li Ye and Sebastian Niepel from the University of Cologne and Kirsi Ziegler at Helsinki University of Technology) analyzed this Enron e-mail dataset (2005). Their work illustrates how a large communication archive can be mined, in this case revealing hidden links and relationships among Enron employees to uncover collusion and fraud by revealing hidden links.

One of Enron's misdeeds took place in 2001. Enron employees introduced an artificial shortage in the California electricity market and subsequently overcharged Californian energy users. The scheme involved "gaming the system" to fix inflated prices. The students at Cologne set out on a quest to find any suspicious patterns of "innovative" activities that corresponded to the game. They analyzed the communication of Tim Belden, a conspiratorial mastermind at Enron who "invented" the scheme, as well as other key players.

Table 8–1 identifies the main players at Enron during the Californian energy crisis.

Table 8-1. Enron actors during the California energy crisis.*

Name	Position at Enron	Comments
Kenneth Lay	Chairman, President and CEO	Led Enron during most of its history.
Jeffrey Skilling	COO and later CEO	Invented "energy trading," which fueled Enron's tremendous growth.
Greg Whalley	President and COO	Took over these positions after Skilling promotions.

Richard Causey	Executive VP, Chief Accounting Officer	Pleaded guilty in December 2005 to a single charge of securities fraud in exchange for a 7-year sentence.
Dave Delainey	Chairman and CEO, Enron Energy	
Richard Shapiro	VP, Regulatory Affairs	
Tim Belden	Head of Portland trading office	Pleaded guilty in October 2002 to conspiracy for his role in exploiting legal loopholes in California to optimize Enron's energy profits.
Mark Haedicke	Managing Director and General Counsel, Enron Wholesale	
Steven J. Kean	VP and Chief of Staff	
Sally Beck	COO, Enron Wholesale	

* This chart is limited to only those Enron personnel who figure in the analysis of e-mail communication during the 2001 California energy scandal.

The students used the TeCFlow software tool (described earlier) for their analysis and to identify potential "suspects." They undertook a large-scale social network analysis in which they judged actors by their closeness to suspicious people, and they searched for clusters of suspicious activity by looking for communication patterns that would suggest Collaborative Innovation Networks gone bad.

The first method was to filter messages with potentially suspicious content and then focus on the social network created by those messages—necessary because suspicious patterns could not be found simply by looking at the *full* communication among all 150 owners of the Enron e-mail boxes, as Figure 8–21 shows. You could hardly find *any* patterns in a cluster of this unintelligible density.

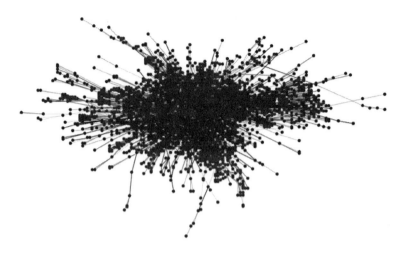

FIGURE 8–21. Full Enron e-mail communication network (150 people, one month).

How, then, do you find the potential "suspects"? Weed out the communication of the "good guys" and you end up with a social network of the "evil" actors and their friends. The students hypothesized that e-mails used to plan or coordinate suspicious actions would contain specific keywords, and so they looked for these suspicious words. They also hypothesized that actors who talk about illegal actions use euphemisms, such as referring to a bomb as a "package." If a criminal context is known, it is possible to search for and filter e-mails that contain words belonging to that particular context. In addition, the relationships between these words can be analyzed to focus further on the context.

An advantage in analyzing the Enron e-mail boxes is that the context in which the suspicious actions were taken is well known. The students used a combination of the following words to select the messages to include in their analysis:

❏ *Affair*—because criminals don't use clear words

❏ *FERC*—which is the Federal Energy Regulatory Commission

◻ *Devastating*—they knew that the investigation would have this effect

◻ *Investigation*—something dangerous, about which to be concerned

◻ *Disclosure*—something to avoid, because of the danger

◻ *Bonus*—additional compensation the subjects would get for pulling off a large deal

Figure 8–22 shows the resulting social network picture of one month of e-mails in 2001, including only messages containing one or more of the above terms. This social network view shows that the actors in Table 8–1 became more central. The filtering process brings these potentially suspicious characters close together.

Next, the students created a concept map of terms used in the filtered dataset. They looked at how the terms were used together in e-mail messages, zooming in on words potentially interesting in a forensic context (Figure 8–23).

The short distance between words such as "confidential," "prohibition," and "delete" allowed the students to identify the messages containing those terms and again look at the social network of the people using those terms. This was done

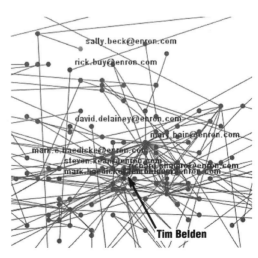

FIGURE 8–22. *Social network of suspicious activities at Enron.*

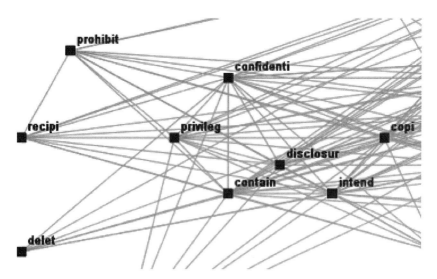

FIGURE 8–23. Concept map of forensically interesting terms in Enron e-mails. (Note: In a process called "stemming," the software tool cuts off the ends of words.)

through the capabilities of the tool, which identified the most significant messages using those terms, as well as the most significant actors using those terms in their e-mail messages. The "significance" was calculated automatically by TeCFlow's statistical analysis of contents and links.

The second method the students employed was a large-scale social network analysis in which they judged actors by their closeness to suspicious people. This narrows the hunt down to include only the most interesting people. They were getting close to proving that birds of feather really *do* flock together—for better or worse.

Figure 8–24 illustrates their approach. We can identify three communities, and we find former Enron COO Jeffrey Skilling positioned in the center of one of them as the leader and connected to the other two.

To discover suspicious people and activities, the students began with known "suspects" and then looked at their interactions with common

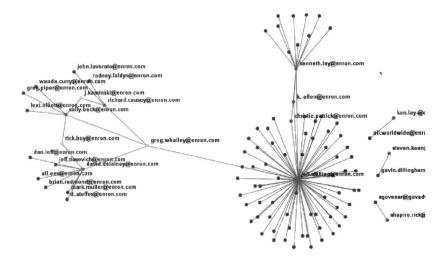

FIGURE 8–24. Jeffrey Skilling is connected to three Enron communities.

friends. In the analysis, a relationship between two actors exists if they have direct e-mail communication. The more e-mails exchanged between two actors, the more intensive is their relationship.

Figure 8–25 illustrates the "common friends" of then Enron CEO Kenneth Lay, later convicted for his role in the collapse of Enron and now deceased, and Tim Belden. Both actors played central roles at Enron during the 2001 Californian energy crisis, but at the time this analysis was done Lay was maintaining that he never knew of the criminal activities of Belden, who pleaded guilty in October 2002 to a federal conspiracy charge for his role in the scheme to drive up California's energy prices. "I did it because I was trying to maximize profit for Enron," Belden told the judge.[8]

While the students found no *direct* connection between Lay and Belden, they did uncover thirteen communication partners they had in common. Of these, six appear in Table 8–1. When we examine this long list of suspicious Enron actors and the topics of their communication, Ken Lay's argument that he knew nothing about the "creative actions" of Tim Belden begins to ring somewhat hollow.

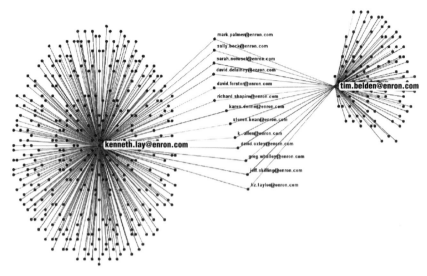

FIGURE 8–25. *"Common friends" of Kenneth Lay and Tim Belden.*

The third method the students used was to search for clusters of suspicious activity by looking for communication patterns that would suggest Collaborative Innovation Networks. Not all innovation is undertaken for good, even if it unfolds in a collaborative context.

In social networking terms, COINs have a very distinctive structure. They develop around a small core group of people over time,

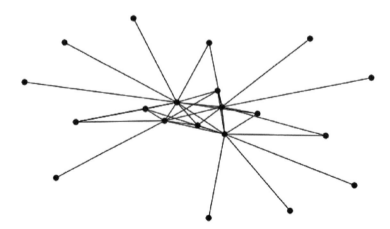

Figure 8-26. A typical COIN networking structure.

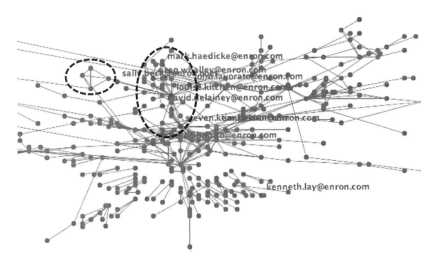

FIGURE 8–27. Two COINs discovered by taking a dynamic view.

and people within that core team are tightly linked. Typically, each individual COIN core member communicates with *all* other core team members; around the core team, we usually find people who are linked only to one or two of the core team members. Figure 8–26 shows a typical COIN networking structure.

With a dataset as large as that containing the Enron e-mails, it can be quite difficult to get a clear overview of the structure of communication with one picture of the entire social network. This problem can be mitigated if a temporal visualization is used that focuses only on a few days at a time. In Figure 8–27, the students generated a picture where the COINs are clearly visible, and nearly all the suspicious people appear in the larger of the two.

This analysis of the Enron mailboxes illustrates how combining the search for COINs and gatekeepers with analysis of discussion content allows compliance analysts and members of the legal community to track emerging trends in e-mail conversations—who is writing to whom, when they're writing, where they're writing from, and what they're writing about. Government, intelligence, and law enforcement professionals can analyze, in near-real time, "conversations" and links between e-mail traffic, blogs, message boards, and other network-based communication, discovering hidden links and emerging trends.

From a more general business perspective, the Enron example of "forensic coolhunting" points to finding patterns of innovation, which are similar whether they are negative (as at Enron) or positive. It's a way to reveal connections that don't quite make sense, and that perhaps warrant a second look in the context of whether you're in "compliance" best practices—to use one of the management world's current buzzwords.

On the positive side, find the healthy patterns of innovation in your company, and you'll probably find your hidden Collaborative Innovation Networks. Find your COINs, and you'll be tapping into the swarm creativity that stimulates trendsetters and trends.

Our final example shows how automated social network analysis can be used for coolfarming—in this case, with an online gaming community as a test bed.

5. Coolfarming a Computer Gaming Community

Marius, one of Peter's students at the University of Cologne, has written a quite popular online strategy game called "Ocean-control." The gaming community includes about 2,000 players, who manage their own islands, controlling resources and building up troops to conquer neighboring islands. Success depends on forming alliances. The more successful players are, the more experience points they earn.

Players communicate with each other through an in-game messaging system, and Marius—together with his friend Daniel—decided to investigate the communication structure of the social

SF   ADAS   CR

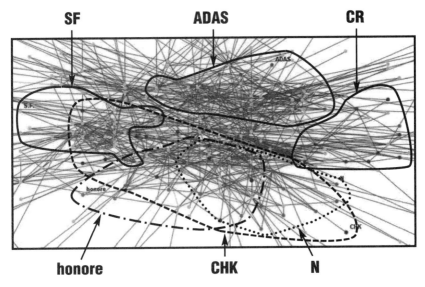

honore   CHK   N

FIGURE 8–28. Alliances as social networks in the "Oceancontrol" online game.

network represented by the Oceancontrol player community.[9] They came up with some cool results. As Figure 8–28 illustrates, they were able to identify clearly—using automated social network analysis— the alliances between the players. Members of an alliance communicate mostly with other members of their alliance, as the figure shows.

The students then looked at what made an alliance particularly successful. It turns out that the alliances that communicated the most with other alliances, embedded in a galaxy structure, were the most successful. Next, the students looked at what made individual players successful, and found that a player's success is directly correlated to the absolute number of virtual friends (direct communication partners), and the absolute number of messages that a player sends and receives. It seems that "balanced" communication behavior, where a player sends and receives approximately the same number of messages, is a further indicator of success.

In a somewhat surprising result, the students also discovered that the number of communication partners matters more than does the absolute number of communications. In other words, in this social network, it is better to have many loose friends than a few close ones.

The students verified their theoretical results by sending out an online-survey to the players. They found that the players had intuitively come to the same conclusions as had Marius and Daniel in their theoretical analysis. For instance, 90 percent of the players responded that they thought communicating a lot within an alliance would make the alliance more successful. Even more interesting, 70 percent of the players reported that they chose new alliance members based on the other players' communication skills, while only 4 percent of the players chose new allies by their success in the game.

Marius and Daniel empirically verified our insights for successful coolfarmers. The first insight is that simply by looking at the social network structure, you can discover the teams (the "alliances" in this example). The second insight is that for a team (a COIN) to be successful, it pays to talk with other teams. The most successful teams are connected to other teams and form galaxies; they don't function as stars. Third, the more friends players (COIN members) have, the more successful they will be. While it helps to have a few strong links to other players, strength of relationship is secondary to the number of links. The best players have a large network of virtual friends, are embedded in different alliances, and send and receive a lot of messages. Marius and Daniel's findings prove one of our main points: Don't be a star, be a galaxy!

Exploring communication archives and using automation to construct a social network based on communication activities between people offers a great way to do coolhunting. People play certain roles within their communities. A gatekeeper connects at least two communities, for instance. A person may function as a leader or as a knowledge expert. The social network graph makes those roles visible. Social network analysis also offers different mathematical, statistical, and graph-theoretical means of finding those people.

The five walk-throughs in this chapter give but a glimpse of how temporal analysis of social networks and communication content can be used for coolhunting. In the next chapter, we put together the pieces and show how you can use not only dynamic social network analysis, but all the principles described in the previous chapters, to become a better coolfarmer and coolhunter yourself.

Five Steps to Becoming a Coolfarmer

In times of change, learners inherit the Earth, while the learned find themselves beautifully equipped to deal with a world that no longer exists.

—Eric Hoffer[1]

WOULDN'T IT be great if you could coolfarm your own ideas? How cool would it be to be able to hunt for trends that you have a hunch might make it, and even help new ideas get over the tipping point? You can even become a better COIN member in the process.

In this chapter, we show how you can become more creative by tapping into the swarm creativity of the people around you. It offers practical, proven steps to being a better communicator and collaborator. You will learn, in particular, how to be a better collaborator in the *virtual* realm. We will explore how you can use electronic means—e-mail, chat, Internet telephony, and videoconferencing—to work together with others more productively. You will also learn how to conduct yourself as a coolhunter, and ultimately, become a coolfarmer.

To follow the process in this chapter, you will need to take a look into a virtual mirror, one that reflects back to you your own communication pattern. The process will work best if you are, or become, a member of a virtual team engaged in an innovation task. Analyzing the communication archive of your team will reveal how much of a coolhunter or even coolfarmer you already are. Here you will see how to change your networking behavior: if it turns out that you are communicating as a star, you'll see how to convert your network into a galaxy.

Over the past few years, we have developed a five-step process to become a better COIN member. It has been presented in seminars and tested in a variety of courses and distributed projects. By reading our book to this point, you've already completed Step 1.

1. Learn about swarm creativity, Collaborative Innovation Networks, and social network analysis.

2. Form a COIN and establish a system to record your own interactions in Step 3, which you will evaluate in Step 4.

3. Coolhunt together with other members of your COIN in an online community of your choice. While coolhunting, record your own interactions for later evaluation in Step 4.

4. After completing Step 3, analyze and measure the collected interactions within your team, looking at the flow of knowledge within the team and the roles of team members.

5. Optimize your own role in your social network so you can become a coolfarmer within your network.

Let's look at each of the steps in detail, using the example of a course Peter taught in Fall 2005. More than two dozen students took the course *simultaneously* on two different campuses: Thirteen students at the Helsinki University of Technology in Finland and twelve students at the University of Cologne in Germany. Peter taught the course jointly with Maria Paasivaara in Helsinki and Detlef Schoder in Cologne. At the time, Maria was earning her Sci.D. degree in Technology in the University's Department of Computer Science and Engineering. Detlef is a professor in Cologne's Department for Information Systems and Information Management. On some occasions, Peter taught remotely from the campus of the Massachusetts Institute of Technology.

The course closely followed the five steps outlined above for becoming a high-performing COIN member. In Step 1, students learned about principles of social network analysis, COINs, and swarm creativity—as you have done in the previous chapters.

In Step 2, students formed seven interdisciplinary teams, each comprising three to four students. All seven teams included students from both Cologne and Helsinki.

Moving to Step 3, each student team chose an online community and applied what they had learned in Step 1 to analyze that community. This allowed them to study online communication in virtual communities other than their own. In particular, students were coolhunting for trends and trendsetters in the online communities they had chosen.

In Step 4, the students analyzed the communication behavior of their own student COIN, based on their online communication record of e-mail, chat, and phone interaction. This allowed them to move to Step 5: by integrating feedback from their peers and examining their own communication records, they improved their online communication behavior and learned to be better online teamworkers and better members of COINs.

How the students in Helsinki and Cologne went through the five steps offers us a practical illustration, a hands-on description of how you can tackle your own conversion to swarm creativity. By following the journey of the students to become coolfarmers, you will be better situated to achieve the same goal.

Step 1: Learn About Swarm Creativity, COINs, and Social Networks

We'll skip a detailed discussion of Step 1. We are confident that, having read our book to this point, you have a good understanding of how social network analysis is used for coolhunting, what swarm creativity is, and what it means to be a galaxy. Chapter 8 showed how an automated social network tool such as TeCFlow can be used to take a peek at your own online communication behavior.[2]

Step 2: Form a COIN

Step 2 involves identifying your own virtual team, which—ideally—will end up operating as a COIN. After you've completed Step 4 (below), you'll be able to determine whether that objective was achieved.

This will require access to the communication archive of a virtual team effort in which you are an active participant. This prerequisite can be met in one of two ways. The easiest is if you already have an electronic archive of a group in which you have been an active member. A simple way to determine whether this is the case is to look at your e-mail folders and document your communication behavior with friends or colleagues with whom you are working on a common task (or with whom you have already completed a task together). Alternatively, you could choose to analyze the mailing list of a community in which you are an active member, such as your place of worship, your programmer's group, a Yahoo group in which you are particularly active, or something similar.

You will also need performance measures for each participant in the collaborative undertaking you choose to analyze. One way is for you to rate the performance of each participant or each participating subteam—smaller groups dedicated to working on a particular task within the larger community. To get more objective ratings, you can ask others for performance ratings of each participant. This has two advantages: First, by getting multiple ratings for each person, potential biases will even out; and second, by including ratings from people who have a greater distance from the rated individual you will also get a more dispassionate assessment. You might also include external performance ratings, such as the number of software bugs fixed, if you analyze a programmer community, or the amount of money brought in by each fundraiser, if you look at a fundraising charity.

If you don't have the communication archive of a group in which you are active, you can set up work on a new collaborative project. Best would be to team up with some friends or colleagues and set a specific objective of analyzing an online community. Let's say you care about new technologies for energy-efficient fuel cells. You and the team you assemble could coolhunt for the latest trends and trendsetting communities in this field, and join one of the communities you found through your coolhunting. The community you join would then be an ideal candidate for analysis.

An easier way to create a new communication archive of a virtual team is to join a Yahoo group of your choice and work with members of the group on a chosen task. If you take this route, you need to become an active member and frequent poster of new messages.

You can't benefit from this lesson in coolfarming if you join a group and then just become a passive lurker—a visitor to an online discussion who reads other people's postings but makes no contribution. This behavior is acceptable while you're searching for a group to join, but not once you've made your decision. If you do join an existing group, we strongly recommend you inform the members of the group about your experiment to analyze the communication archive up front. Others in the group may even want to team with you in doing the analysis, giving you the opportunity to form a true COIN. That would be cool.

As you will in Step 4, to evaluate your own inter-group communication records you will need to make sure that all that communication is recorded automatically. One way to do this is to use e-mail exclusively for communication, since automated evaluation of e-mail is relatively easy. If the team members work together face-to-face on some occasions, you can send a reminder e-mail to the participant mailing list and thus keep track of these interactions.

In the course at Cologne and Helsinki, the students had never met their colleagues in the other city face-to-face. So, they first had to form virtual teams and then do joint projects to collect electronic communication records of their work.

In a first full team meeting, held virtually, students introduced themselves to colleagues in the same classroom, and via videoconferencing to peers in the remote location. Teams then self-organized based on their preferences for certain topics for study that were suggested. Team formation took two to three days of exchanging e-mails among students in Helsinki and Cologne and the instructors. In the end, there were seven bi-located teams. As the team members were geographically distributed, their communication was conducted online, mostly by e-mail. Each team selected an online community for analysis. Four of them will be familiar to you from Chapter 8: Wikinews, the eCoustics forum, and Enron employee e-mails.

We asked the students to send copies of all their team-related e-mails to one of seven dummy e-mail project addresses where each team's communication could be archived for use in Step 4. We also offered a Wiki as a forum for discussion. Chat and Skype were used heavily for communication. Students working at the same location also met face-to-face.

Step 3: Coolhunt in an Online Community

In Step 3, you create an electronic communication archive documenting your online collaboration behavior in a virtual team. Together with the members of your virtual team, you will now be coolhunting for trends and trendsetters in the online community you chose in Step 2. You'll communicate with the people in that online community. You'll also need to understand the context of the community, which requires some research—for instance, you can read up about the community and its topic on the Web and in other media. To analyze and understand the social networking structure of the community, you have access to a powerful tool: dynamic social network analysis (discussed in Chapter 8).

In preparation for Step 4, be sure to record *all* the interactions with the group, be it postings to a newsgroup, online forum, or mailing list, or direct interaction through e-mail, chat, or face-to-face communication with other group members.

In our course in Cologne and Helsinki, students collected copies of all their communication during the four-week projects in which they analyzed communities such as Wikinews, the Enron e-mail archive, and the eCoustics forum. This allowed them to build a single, combined e-mail database for later analysis with the TeCFlow tool.

Because the topic of their projects was analyzing an online community, students had a prime opportunity to study good and bad communication behavior and apply the coolhunting principles they had learned in Step 1. At the end of the project, each team produced a final report, which included results and first lessons learned about virtual collaboration. Each team then presented its results to the other six teams in a videoconference presentation. We asked each team to have at least one presenter from Cologne and from Helsinki.

Performance evaluation is key to improving your online communication and, thus, key to coolhunting and coolfarming in online communities. In preparation for Step 4, there needs to be a performance evaluation of each individual participant and each subteam (if there are any). These ratings will be used in Step 4 to identify the best communication behavior for the most productive COIN members.

When the coolhunting period—lasting from a few days to a few weeks—is over, you should also rate your own performance as well as the performance of your virtual team members as virtual collaborators. If you decided to do an analysis of your collaboration in a Yahoo group, you ideally will have informed your virtual team members beforehand of your intent to use your participation in the group to analyze your own coolhunting and coolfarming behavior. You could then ask your virtual team members to rate you.

When we have done this exercise in the past, we have tried a variety of ways to do ratings. You could, for example, invite one or more senior members of the community to rate performance parameters such as how much trust in your contributions they developed over time, how much standing or prestige your contributions and overall behavior garnered, and the overall value they assigned to your contributions. These ratings could be done for individuals as well as for subteams working together on a dedicated task within the larger community. Senior members of a community doing the rating could be the administrators of the Yahoo group mailing list, or the project leaders of the open-source project in which you participated, or the coordinators of the online forum on fuel cells where you have been a very active member. You could then ask those senior members whom they trust most within their community, rating all members of their community or who they think has the highest prestige within the community, or who they think has contributed the most to the community goals.

The approach we took to rating performance in the course at Helsinki and Cologne offers a detailed example of how to accomplish this task. We decided to do the course performance evaluations in true swarm creativity—not by the instructors but by the students themselves. So, after the project presentations, each student graded the quality of the work of the teams other than her or his own on a scale from 1 to 4, with 1 being the best grade. The quality of the work of each team was ranked based on the quality of the final presentation of the team and the final report. Students also ranked the quality of the individual contribution of their own team members: Each student gave a grade to each of the six other teams as well as to his or her peers within a team.

Step 4: Measure Communication in Your Own COIN

In Step 4, you analyze your own communication behavior to determine whether you are behaving like a star or a galaxy. You should then correlate the performance measurements of all individuals and teams—including your own—with their communication patterns. This can be done by loading your communication data into a social network analysis tool such as TeCFlow to generate communication

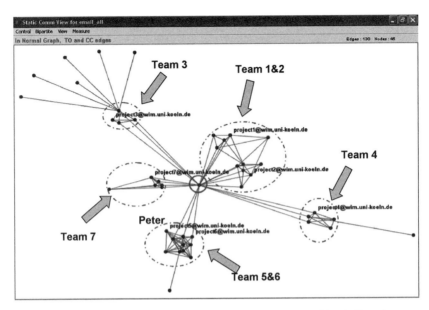

FIGURE 9–1. *Communication patterns of project teams while working in Step 4.*

pictures and movies. Figure 9–1 shows an example of what these pictures and movies will look like, taken from the analysis of student projects at Helsinki and Cologne.

From our experience with the course, three main principles of good communication behavior became apparent. The first is that *it pays to communicate between subteams*.

Figure 9–1 reveals the social network among the students during this period. Ties between the students and the teacher were exposed by mining the e-mail archive of communication during the course. As this was a course about swarm creativity, students had been encouraged to collaborate not just within their teams, but also to tap into knowledge networks of the other students who were not on their teams. Figure 9–1 illustrates that the goal was not reached.

Note the central role of Peter, the instructor, with very little inter-team communication. Only Teams 1 & 2 and Teams 5 & 6 show inter-team communication. This is not how it should be, and it was one of the major lessons of the course. Analyzing your own communication structure, you will quickly see whether your community collaborates as a collection of stars or as a galaxy.

The second main principle of good communication behavior we learned from the course is straightforward: Overall, you should *communicate a lot*. After looking at the social network, we examined simple communication parameters such as the number of e-mails sent within each team. As our first metric, we found that *number* of e-mails sent within a team mattered. The teams with the highest volume of communication received higher ratings than the teams where everyone worked in isolation, and team members exchanged little e-mail with each other. The lesson is clear: it pays to lead team-wide discussions about project-specific issues.

The next metric is the "balance" in communication behavior. In a perfectly "balanced" team, each member will send and receive the same number of messages, distributed evenly over time. In our course, we counted the numbers of messages each student sent to other students on his or her team, and also looked at how balanced this behavior was within the teams. For instance, did one person send a significantly greater number of e-mails than did other team members? Were there team members who were much more passive than the rest of the group with respect to e-mail communication? And how did this behavior change over the four-week duration of the project?

The principle that emerged is this: *Display "balanced" communication behavior.* Balanced internal communication will lead to better productivity in your COIN. In our course, we found that external ratings, where the performance of one team was judged by the other teams, showed a high correlation with the balance of a team's communication. There was strong statistical proof that teams in which there were no lurkers and in which everyone contributed relatively equally, had better performance. We could not confirm this for team-internal ratings, however. We had expected that teams with balanced behavior, in which everyone was pulling her or his weight, would have a higher average team-internal rating. We could not confirm this hypothesis, although we had empirical evidence that it was true. We concluded that external ratings were more honest than the internal ones as students were not asked to rate team members they had been working with closely for the last four weeks on the same project. External ratings were more precise, too, as they were based on a larger number of rankings.

As one of their main takeaways, students found that it pays to work together—internal evaluation by team members and external evaluation of the team's output by other groups are correlated.[3] The better rating a team's work was given by other students outside of the team, the better team members rated the contribution of each other within a team. We should point out that these ratings were done anonymously. Joe had absolutely no way of knowing whether Bill had given him a high or low rating. Therefore, students had no incentive to "be nice to one other" in their ratings. Nevertheless, satisfied teams applying all the principles of swarm creativity gave good mutual ratings to team members and provided work of good quality. This shows that it pays to work together as a COIN!

Step 5: Become a Coolfarmer

Step 5 is your chance to apply the insights you gained when correlating your own communication behavior with your group's performance to improve your future communication behavior and collaboration style in COINs. Our work suggests communicating helps: There can never be too much communication! And talk in galaxies, and not as stars! The more teams talked internally, the better they performed. We also found that participants of teams exhibiting balanced communication behavior perform best.

In the Cologne and Helsinki course, students began to coolfarm their own research. They became collaborative innovators themselves, coming up with many ideas for improving the course. And, in true self-organization, they formed their own galaxies. For example, in the final class presentation, two teams decided to merge their efforts, forming a larger COIN in which they condensed their own ideas for "working together as a social network," as they called it. Of the seven student projects, seven follow-up research projects were identified. Three months after the course ended, three scientific papers had been written and submitted to academic conferences,[4] and other online communities were analyzed for two diploma theses.

Not all of the follow-up projects were done by the same team members as in the course; new team configurations emerged and subject areas were shifting. This is true swarm creativity, where COINs form, grow, and evolve in many different forms. Student participation was entirely voluntary and intrinsically motivated. No student was paid as a research assistant or received studying credit for writing the scientific papers.

As the students found, knowing about social network analysis at a theoretical level gets you only so far toward becoming a successful coolhunter and coolfarmer. The difficult task is its application. Without feedback from their colleagues, particularly their team members in another location, they would not have been able to make a fundamental shift in their traditional communication behavior and themselves become coolfarmers.

If you try this experiment and go through the five steps we've detailed in this chapter, we think you'll arrive at the same conclusion as did the students in the course. They told us that this was one of the difficult and most work-intensive courses they had ever taken, but one that they believed would forever change the way they worked with others. As one student told Peter, "The most valuable thing I learned was that the better communication is, the more successful you are—personally or as a team."

Communication is a prime ingredient in honing your coolhunting and coolfarming skills. In our final chapter, we lay out the path for joining a swarming world of creativity and innovation!

10

The Coming World of Swarm Creativity

We know what we are, but know not what we may be.

—William Shakespeare[1]

IN OUR EXAMPLES from the business world in previous chapters, we've been pointing to two different worlds. One is where most business people reside. It's a world in which actions are driven by the quest for profit and market share. It's a world of quarterly accounting where interim and yearly results make or break individuals and companies. In that world, the share price at the end of each day is what matters most.

We call that the old world. Organizations in the old world are hierarchical, with command-and-control structures that grew up in the early days of industry and have since become yokes around the necks of innovation. It is not a world of swarm creativity.

Other examples we've used are of a *new swarming* world. Google gives a day a week to its employees to do nothing but swarm together and come up with ideas, and cool products have emerged. Google is a new world company, but few would argue that Google's business model hasn't achieved some pretty remarkable results by the old world standards.

Of course, the differentiation between these two worlds isn't black and white, cut and dried. In many (perhaps most) large companies, for instance, you can find groups of creative individuals swarming together to explore ideas about which they care deeply, irrespective of any direct or immediate connection to the bottom line. These are the hidden COINs that are not being nurtured, the activities that are *cool* but never given the space to flourish.

Morphing into Swarm Creativity

Lots of companies sit on the cusp of the two worlds, with a hybrid form of organization that serves them well when it comes to creativity, coolhunting, and coolfarming. Starbucks is a good example.

STARBUCKS THE TRENDSETTER

We're not sure which of the many trends associated with Starbucks were coolhunted or coolfarmed. It doesn't really matter. The point is that there *are* so many trends that trace back to Starbucks in some way. Teenagers and adults alike, for instance, are drinking huge quantities of "Chai tea" at Starbucks locations across the United States. How many of you can even remember such a thing as "Chai tea" from *your* teen years?

Chai is simply the Hindi word for "tea" (and the word for tea in quite a few other Asian languages). Starbucks either found a trend simmering somewhere in the United States and ran with it, or created the trend itself—taking the milky, slightly spicy variety known as *masala chai* in India and bringing it to a huge U.S. market.

Starkbucks is a good example of this hybrid of old and new worlds. It is notorious for having had one or more rather "difficult" chief marketing officers in the past decade, and the organization has plenty of hierarchy to go around. And yet, Starbucks has also figured out ways to unleash swarm creativity. At its corporate headquarters, for one example, it has created the Starbucks Creative Group, which brainstorms how to articulate the Starbucks brand. Most people in the group are former *baristas*—the word Starbucks uses to describe the people who make and serve you your coffee—and chai—in the local shops.

In 2004, *Howdesign.com*, a highly regarded online magazine, awarded the Starbucks Creative Group its "In-House Design Group of the Year" Award. Thomas Powell, one of the group members, told the magazine where the creativity comes from:

> Because so many of us started as baristas, we kind of view ourselves as the keepers of this tribal knowledge. I started here in 1990, before the big Starbucks explosion, and what intrigued me about this company was that they took something that was mundane—coffee—and made it interesting and exciting again.[2]

Powell calls it "tribal knowledge." We call it swarm creativity. Powell describes taking something mundane and making it exciting and interesting. We call it coolfarming.

There's a lot of evidence that even companies that tend to think according to the old-world norms, and are organized that way, are altering their behavior to greater or lesser degrees to correspond to the new world. Some of them are even world leaders in innovation.

IBM DONATES PATENTS TO THE SWARM

Take IBM, a company that receives more U.S. patents—by very far—than any other private-sector organization in the world, and has done so for more than a dozen years.[3] In January 2005, IBM announced that it would donate 500 of its patents for free use by software developers. The patents are in simultaneous multiprocessing, image processing, database management, storage management, e-commerce, and networking. The one condition was that the projects of programmers who use them must meet the Open Source Initiative definition of open-source software.[4] The move, according to IBM executives, was aimed at spurring technological innovation and spurring other companies to unlock their own patents in order to create what IBM refers to as "patent commons"—similar to shared public lands.

Why would IBM take such a step? It flies in the face of what rivals such as Microsoft say—that open-source software development is an assault on corporate intellectual property rights. And it also puts IBM in a much different camp from some of its biggest customers, such as pharmaceutical companies and media giants, which are among the most ardent defenders of patents.

We don't think it's unadulterated altruism. We don't think IBM has suddenly decided to follow our swarm creativity model. Rather, it's a sign of the reconfiguration of how innovation "gets done best" that we've been talking about. Even a company like IBM sees the sea change represented by the success of new world companies that have gained their power by giving it away. The power IBM hopes to gain? "As the leading provider of computer services," writes Reuters, "IBM also stands to benefit from helping other companies make use of new technology developed under the open licensing program."[5] Procter & Gamble, another old world company, has adopted what one publication identifies as an "open-source innovation strategy" through its "Connect and Develop" model. Through this model, P&G "embrace[s] the collective brains of the world" and "tap[s] networks of inventors, scientists, and suppliers for new products that can be developed in-house."[6] The company makes some remarkable claims about how it has benefited, attributing a nearly 60 percent growth in R&D productivity from what we see as a form of swarm creativity.[7] Still other companies that have started out like those in the old world are morphing even more into new world companies, or at least increasingly exhibiting the new world characteristics. Cisco Systems is a good example.

CISCO SYSTEMS TAPS INTO SWARM CREATIVITY

We spoke to Douglas Frosst, senior manager for Executive Thought Leadership at Cisco.[8] He described his company's approach to coolhunting, and how Cisco is tapping into swarm creativity. He had also read Peter's previous book, so he used some of our language.

First he described the wide-ranging network of personal links Cisco has established with people around the world. These are people Cisco can discuss things with. They have their own executives sit on the boards of other companies. They have extensive relationships with venture capitalists, and they ask them what they're seeing, what's taking off, and what they're investing in. Some VCs sit on Cisco's executive committee. The company also invests an enormous amount of effort to get customer input, not just about Cisco products and the customers' technology issues but about trends and challenges generally in business. Then there are the personal networks. According to Frosst:

> We get a galaxy effect from this web of relationships. We don't rely on any *single* source of information, but we pay attention to all these different inputs. We prefer the model of less-

focused ideas put out on the table for discussion with a group
of people, and less-formal, more general associations.

Cisco, like many other technology companies, is also mining the
academic world. They find this to be a good source for ideas and
acquisitions. But Cisco has a different approach from many firms
that are roaming the halls of places like MIT (we see this all the
time) looking for an "invention" in a laboratory. While most other
sponsors flesh out projects, setting specific research goals and identifying deliverables by the MIT researchers to the sponsor at agreed-
upon milestones, Cisco sponsors "partnerships" with different
groups at Stanford, MIT, and elsewhere, but doesn't like putting a
specific objective for the company in front of people. The company
fears it might limit the results. "Our expectation," says Frosst, "is
that hanging out with a diverse and cross-functional group of smart
people who are looking at issues" will pay dividends.

No one would argue that Cisco doesn't care about its share price,
profits, and bottom line, but the kind of behavior Frosst describes
speaks to a more coolhunting-oriented approach to growth than we
usually see in large companies. We asked Frosst to describe the
Cisco culture that drives this approach, and his answer corresponded
to many of the ideas we've stated in previous chapters. Among other
things, he pointed to a focus on teamwork and open communication,
the conscious rejection of what he calls a "technology religion" that
any one technology or protocol is better than another; and a specific focus on market transitions.

At Cisco, there is less focus on individual stars. It's all about the
galaxies. When considering an acquisition, the company cares more
about the leadership team than about the technology. Cisco is coolfarming its acquisitions in the same way Robert Langer and John
Doerr are coolfarming their startups. Unlike in their work, though,

at Cisco it isn't an individual like CEO John Chambers who makes the decision about acquisitions. That decision power, in true swarm creativity, is delegated to the business unit that would integrate the acquired company or technology.

Like Peter's friend Wayne, whom you met in Chapter 5, Cisco is coolhunting for new acquisition opportunities by looking for galaxies. The company does this through personal networking, conversations with customers, and its academic research partnerships. "One of the techniques we use throughout the company in all areas is to be aware of potential market transition opportunities, whether driven by disruptive technology, the value chain in a particular market, business process change, or geographic or geopolitical change—and not be negatively affected by them," explained Frosst. Cisco is searching for trends, like any good coolhunter would do.

Cisco even unleashed swarm creativity through what looks to us very much like a COIN as it developed the "interactions" concept that is at the core of the company's engagements with business decision makers. As part of its corporate vision, Cisco established the idea that future productivity gains will come not just from technology and cost reduction, but also from "adding value to the exchange of information" through "the interactions between colleagues, partners, and customers."[9] This idea ties in perfectly with the key message of our book—that by swarming together and creating new social networks, tremendous value will be set free.

When John Chambers, Cisco's CEO, wanted to take this concept that was being developed in-house to a higher level and promulgate it beyond Cisco's walls, he went to his executive team. They in turn brought in a diverse group of people from throughout the company's various organizations and units not only to brainstorm the potential paths, but also to discuss what people were hearing from customers, the academic community, and others in the "galaxy" Frosst described.

What evolved was a COIN, triggered from the top down but that took on a life of its own. Self-organizing and outside the hierarchical boundaries of Cisco, it extended into many different business units. Within a few months, the COIN redefined Cisco's corporate message. By most measures, it has been highly successful, producing a set of strategic messages converted into white papers and quarterly newsletters that have been instrumental in reshaping the external perception of Cisco.

We don't want to imply with this example that typical command-and-control organizations, by contrast, are completely lacking in innovative activity. For a counterexample, look at the invention of the transistor at strictly hierarchical Bell Laboratories, or the U.S. Naval Research Lab discovering the radar. Those were radical innovations of the last century. We posit that the most radical—and also many more transformative—innovations of our new century will be made by self-organizing Collaborative Innovation Networks.

Stakeholders or Shareholders?

The coolhunting and swarm creativity we advocate are predicated on a fundamental rejection of the central tenets of a perspective that has come to be known as "shareholder value." We believe that success in the new world requires discarding the old-world precepts that come with the trader's mentality on which shareholder value is based. Short-term gains and even quick riches may accrue to those who buy low and sell high. But how will you ever compete like that in a new world where innovators give away power by giving their inventions away for free? How can you wage a competitive war on the battlefield of profit when your competitor doesn't care about profit?

It's a frightening prospect. Richard Siklos describes the "friendly menaces"—the growing number of new media ventures that "leave the competition scratching their heads because they don't really aim to compete in the first place: their creators are merely taking advantage of the economics of the online medium to do something that they feel good about."[10] These ventures are "not in it for the money"—but we've shown that they can quickly become financial juggernauts because of their embrace of the new-world principles.

Siklos cites a number of examples that are making old-worlders shake in their boots. There's the Firefox browser, given away free online and stealing "market share" from Microsoft's Internet Explorer. Firefox is nonprofit, but Google pays Mozilla—a self-described "open-source community of [software] developers and testers"—to be the Firefox search engine. Google itself was one of the early examples of the kinds of ventures Siklos describes.

Craigslist.org is another of Siklos' example—"mostly a free listings service that acts as a community resource." If you've ever used Craigslist, you probably marvel at the breadth and depth of this resource. Scott found his editorial/research assistant Maya (she's mentioned in our acknowledgments) through Craigslist. Scott's older daughter, when she moved across the country, ran out of time but still had a lot of good stuff from her apartment to give away. She put it all in a secure but not easily visible spot outside her building, posted a notice on Craigslist, and within 24 hours everything had been snatched up by people who needed things. Plus, they left the place nice and clean.

A former employee of Craigslist, who owned a 25 percent stake in the company, sold it to eBay in 2005. eBay already understand the new-world way of linking people together—in its case, buyers and sellers—through transparency and giving power away.

Craigslist doesn't focus on its handful of shareholders, but adopts a stakeholder value perspective. We think this is a common feature of many of the COIN-operated, swarm creativity business examples we've highlighted in this book. Coolhunting and coolfarming, too, benefit from the stakeholder value perspective. Let's look at their differences.

A focus on *shareholder value* is definitely of the old world. The *owners* of an organization are the drivers, and success is measured by profitability, share price, and dividends. Sure, shareholders matter, but their interests—as members of society—are ultimately served best by economic efficiency and conditions that allow everyone to pursue whatever works best for them and is in their own self-interest.

Stakeholders include the swarm—anyone who can affect or is affected by an action. From a business perspective, that includes employees, shareholders, suppliers, customers, and even competitors. It also includes people in the community, regulators and other government agencies, and—depending on your business—fish in the sea, birds in the sky, or squirrels in the park. The stakeholder perspective can be very broad, indeed. And it benefits from the notion that success comes from constructing "win-win" scenarios in which everyone gets something positive.

That's a lot like the principles of coolhunting and swarm creativity we've been espousing, writ on a large scale. Here they are again, in Table 10–1.

Table 10-1. Coolfarming and coolhunting.

Coolfarming	Coolhunting
Gain power by giving it away	Search for COINs and self-organizing teams
Seed community with idea	Search for ideas
Mandate intrinsic motivation	Search for intrinsically motivated people
Recruit trendsetters	Search for trendsetters

It's very cool to be a coolhunter, but it's even more cool to be a coolfarmer—like Benjamin Franklin, Robert Langer, or Peter's publisher friend Wayne. We've said it several times in this book: When it comes to coolhunting, coolfarming, and swarm creativity, the best illustrations come from the world of the bees. From the hive, we can extract more than honey from four key behaviors that you should internalize to be a coolhunter and, even better, a coolfarmer.

Immerse Yourself in the Swarm

Coolhunters immerse themselves in the swarm. What does that mean? Let's look first at the bees.

Master beekeepers are in sync with the bees. They watch the hives every day. They know just when the bees need to be fed. They can do almost anything with the bees and avoid getting stung. They understand beekeeping as anticipation, not just reaction.

From a business point of view, immersing yourself in the swarm means being not only a beekeeper but also a bee. There are many examples of ambitious managers killing swarm creativity by trying to usurp the output of a Collaborative Innovation Network or by hijacking its leadership. Just look at how long it took for the hypertext concept to take off, from the time it was first suggested (with a different name) in 1945 by Vannevar Bush.[11] The U.S. Navy used a hypertext system called ZOG in 1982 to manage online documentation on the aircraft carrier Carl Vinson.[12] But the system was still held under wraps in the hierarchical Navy bureaucracy. It wasn't until the hypertext concept was used at CERN[13]—an open environment where people were already collaborating in COINs—that this tool changed our world by finally taking off and spreading globally.

Listen to the Swarm

Coolhunters listen to the swarm. It's how they know when a new trend is emerging.

Master beekeepers can tell from listening to the bees whether they are up to something. When they are about to create a new swarm, the pitch changes in the hive. The new swarm means a new community of bees, and double the output. Beekeepers benefit by being on their toes, ready the moment the new swarm emerges from the hive and sets up its own hive. Beekeepers who miss this moment may never find the new hive. You have to be "with" the swarm at the moment it's flying. But if beekeepers have been actively involved in nurturing their bees, they receive something of great value in return: when the bees swarm and create a new hive, the output for the beekeeper is doubled.

In the business world, listen to the swarm and it will tell you when a new trend is emerging. Listen to the swarm with extra care, and you'll know just the moment to act. Windows of opportunity are very short in today's world of technology-driven innovation. Clayton Christensen, in *The Innovator's Dilemma*, devotes an entire chapter to the tremendous shake-up in the hard disk industry.[14] It came largely from existing firms being caught napping. Big players missed the big shift because they weren't listening to the swarm creativity in the industry and, sometimes, to the COINs within their own walls.

A lot of this failure came when big companies were so invested in the way they were doing business—and the specific technology associated with their bit of the marketplace—that they were unable to make any adjustments in time, even if they had been listening.

Contrast this with the example of Cisco. The company trusts swarm creativity and its Collaborative Innovation Networks. Cisco empowers its researchers to think and do, and gets out of the way.

As Douglas Frosst of Cisco explained to us, it's best to avoid limiting the potential results of swarm creativity.[15] The objective is to be there when the swarm comes up with a great idea, catch it, and make something of it—not usurp it.

The business examples of being caught napping because they weren't listening to the swarm are many, and run the gamut from large-scale debacles to relatively simple fixes.

There are the banks in Thailand that fell way behind their foreign competitors in offering consumer credit to local customers in one of the world's fastest-growing markets for consumer credit. While Citibank, HSBC, and other banks based in the West were busy courting newly "enriched" people in Thailand working in that country's growing high-tech sector, the local banks—who had access to the swarms in their own institutions that were also seeking credit cards—at first missed this opportunity.

The Thai banks are playing catch-up, but at least it's something they have a good chance of achieving. Sometimes the failure to listen to the swarm can be considerably more costly. Take, for example, Digital Equipment Corporation (DEC) and the introduction of the personal computer. DEC's charismatic CEO, Ken Olsen— by many accounts very supportive of COINs—completely missed listening to the swarms when it came to PCs. He thought he knew what his customers wanted, and he failed to listen to them and to his own employees. As the marketplace left DEC behind, Olsen had his company continue to build better and faster microcomputers and technologically sophisticated, but nonstandard, personal computers that customers simply didn't accept.

DEC paid a heavy price for Olsen not listening to the swarm. A shell of its former self, the company was gobbled up by Compaq, and is now part of Hewlett-Packard.

Trust the Swarm

Delegate power to the swarm and get out of the way. Let the swarm do its thing, and reap the benefits. This is a critically important part of what a successful coolfarmer does.

Again, let's look at beekeeping. One of the key principles of beekeeping is to maintain optimal conditions for the bees. The beekeeper nurtures the bee culture, ensuring that the bees enjoy the conditions that enable the swarm to do its work. Beekeepers try to keep away the wasps so the bees don't have to sacrifice themselves for the swarm—recognizing all the while that the bees, like good members of a Collaborative Innovation Network—are altruistic (in the case of the bees, they'll give their lives to protect the swarm). Beekeepers keep away other honey-loving predators, like bears. Beekeepers move the hives when necessary.

In a nutshell, the beekeeper does whatever is necessary to ensure that the swarm can do its most important work—*make honey*. And it's about the swarm *continuing* to make honey. The perspective is long-term and sustainable, not short-term.

In the business world, trusting the swarm is just as important. Coolfarmers know that to benefit, that for a trend to "pay off," they must find a way to let the swarm do what the swarm feels is the right thing. Managers who pull the plug on swarm creativity when the swarm seems to be doing something that runs counter to short-term interests are making a big mistake.

In the late 1970s, the global swarm of innovation in automobiles was pummeling America's shores. This was before the U.S. landscape was dotted with auto plants owned by foreign-based companies. Japan was consistently producing cars and light trucks that got better gas mileage and had far superior maintenance profiles than U.S. vehicles. The key word here is "producing." U.S. automakers had the know-how to match the Japanese efforts; the creative swarms inside of the "Big Three" automakers Ford, General Motors, and Chrysler were all talking about fuel efficiency, and calling for their bosses to make the investment. The swarm was on the right track, but the bosses would have nothing to do with "producing" these vehicles. No, Detroit had its heart set on a different set of products.

Arrogant old-world thinking on the part of the senior executives at the Big Three, colluding with the U.S. government, took the story off the swarm's track and down a much different road. If you were a taxpayer at the time, you paid dearly for the refusal of these people to listen to the swarm. And we all pay dearly today.

Chrysler was in particular trouble, on the brink of bankruptcy. Congress came to the rescue with $1.5 billion in federal loan guarantees to save the company. And President Carter imposed a 25 percent tariff on imports of light trucks from Japan—"building a protective wall around what were to become Detroit's hottest products: sport utility vehicles and minivans."[16] The next administration continued on the same path.

The big news today in the U.S. auto industry as of our writing is that General Motors and Ford are gasping for air. Chrysler has long since merged with a German company. Gas prices are rising, and a lot of American consumers are stuck with SUVs that cost a fortune to keep on the road. U.S. automakers are still worrying about protecting their "turf."

Our point in mentioning the auto industry is not to debate the issues of Japan's reputed manipulation of currency to bolster its carmakers' chances in external markets, or to take a stand on protectionism. We don't think our opinion matters on whether artificially low gas prices in the United States are to blame for the current dilemma, and we aren't going to warn about another bailout of a giant U.S. corporation. We just want to pose a simple, rhetorical question:

Where would the U.S. car industry be today if it had listened to its own swarms?

Share with the Swarm

If you take everything from the swarm that the swarm creates, you're nothing like a coolfarmer. Just imagine what would have happened to the World Wide Web if the U.S. Patent Office had upheld the claim made by British Telecom that it owned the intellectual property rights to the Web's underlying hypertext concept. BT had filed for a patent in 1976, but only discovered its potential applicability to the Web in 1989.[17] Fortunately for all of us, a U.S. Federal Court ruled against BT, accepting the argument that Ted Nelson and Douglas Engelbart had pioneered the same concepts long before they were part of BT's patent. Had the court case gone in the other direction, we might all be paying royalties to British Telecom, and the universal capability the Web affords us to share information with the world for free would be crippled—*fatally*.

Beekeepers know that when it comes time to reap the honey harvest, they must leave some behind. The bees like honey, too. Leave some behind, or the swarm will die. And when the swarm of bees is in its "uncreative" time, too, they must still be fed. In the winter, they need to be fed some sugar, or they won't survive. And ensuring that the swarm survives into the future, to create anew, is the key to continued collaboration.

The same principle applies in the business world. In a Collaborative Innovation Network, the members work altruistically because of their shared interest in whatever they're creating. The smart coolfarmer shares with the swarm, ensuring that when something profitable comes of that swarm creativity the swarm members get an opportunity to profit, too.

Bees can survive only on sugar, but they have no motivation to do so. They want some of their own honey—the honey they produce. Similarly, reinvesting in the business swarm pays dividends.

The overarching theme is to *nurture* swarm creativity and collaborative innovation. Coolhunters find the trends, and coolfarmers nurture the trends and trendsetters.

With the caveats from our swarm madness discussion (Chapter 6), the lesson is to look to the bees. Is it swarm creativity? Well, if it looks like the bees, the answer is probably yes. Is it genuinely collaborative innovation, done for the right reasons, with the right motivations, and—we argue—thus likely to ensure the desired outcome. Well, if it looks like the bees, if people are self-sacrificing for the good of the creative act, the answer is probably yes.

In the Collaborative Innovation Network at Deloitte Consulting (discussed in Chapter 4), Tom sacrificed his own short-term career for the good of the swarm. He would have been promoted much sooner, but for a year he worked in swarm creativity rather than on a much higher-profile billable project. Tom was a coolfarmer and a bee all wrapped in one.

Take these lessons to heart, and you can be a coolhunter and even a coolfarmer. Embrace swarm creativity, and you can collaborate with others to develop the next big idea, for all the right reasons. Apply the principles and you are well on your way to finding the next cool investment. Follow the example of John Doerr, and you'll uncover the cool teams that work well together and point the way to the trends.

The business model that makes the most sense, that corresponds to our new high-speed, networked, digital world, is the one where the Benjamin Franklins outpace the old-world thinkers. Which race will you run?

NOTES

FOREWORD

1. Hugo Liu, Pattie Maes, and Glorianna Davenport, "Unraveling the Taste Fabric of Social Networks," *International Journal on Semantic Web and Information Systems* 2,1 (2006): 42-71. http://mf.media.mit.edu/pubs/journal/TasteFabric.pdf

INTRODUCTION

1. Malcolm Gladwell, *The Tipping Point: How Little Things Can Make a Big Difference* (Boston: Little, Brown, 2000).

2. http://www.pbs.org/wgbh/pages/frontline/shows/cool/interviews/gladwell.html

3. See, for example: http://www.coolhunting.com

4. We owe a nod to the expression "swarm intelligence," introduced in a 1989 paper on cellular robotics. Swarm intelligence is a technique for artificial intelligence that is based on the study of collective behavior in self-organized, decentralized systems. See G. Beni and J. Wang, "Swarm Intelligence," in *Proceedings of the Seventh Annual Meeting of the Robotics Society of Japan* (Tokyo: RSJ Press, 1989), pp. 425-428.

5. Peter Gloor, *Swarm Creativity—Competitive Advantage through Collaborative Innovation Networks* (New York: Oxford University Press, 2006).

CHAPTER 1

1. William Gibson, *Pattern Recognition* (New York: G.P. Putnam & Sons, 2003).

2. Susan Stellin, "On Board the Message Board," *New York Times*, June 14, 2005.

3. http://investor.google.com/conduct.html

4. http://www.google.com/support/jobs/bin/static.py?page=about.html

5. Eric von Hippel, *Democratizing Innovation* (Cambridge, Mass.: The MIT Press, 2005).

6. Bryce Ryan and Neal C. Gross, "The Diffusion of Hybrid Seed Corn in Two Iowa Communities," *Rural Sociology* 13 (March 1943): 15-24.

7. Everett M. Rogers, *Diffusion of Innovation* (New York: Free Press, 1962).

8. Bob Metcalfe, "Metcalfe's Law: A Network Becomes More Valuable as It Reaches More Users," *Infoworld*, Oct. 2, 1995.

9. David P. Reed, "The Law of the Pack," *Harvard Business Review*, February 2001, pp. 23-24.

10. There is a rich and growing body of research on the role of network effects in finding trends and even forecasting how innovations will diffuse. For a good example, see Detlef Schoder, "Forecasting the Success of Telecommunication Services in the Presence of Network Effects," *Information Economics and Policy* 12 (2000): 181-200.

CHAPTER 2

1. http://www.linuxweb.com/lw_quotes.html

2. The 14th Dalai Lama, "The Medicine of Altruism," at: http://www.dalailama.com/page.65.htm

3. http://www.wipo.int/ipstats/en/statistics/patents/top_countries.html

4. http://news.com.com/eBay+to+nab+Skype+for+2.6+billion/2100-1030_35860055.html

5. *The Wall Street Transcript*, "Company Interview: Darren Carroll, InnoCentive, Inc.," at: http://www.twst.com/notes/articles/abh103.html

6. Richard Springer, "InnoCentive Hosts the World's Largest Virtual Laboratory," *India West* 30, 25 (April 29, 2005).

7. William C. Taylor, "Here's an Idea: Let Everyone Have Ideas," *New York Times*, Sunday Business, March 26, 2006, p. Bu-3.

8. Ali Hussein, "It's All About Talent 24/7," ZDNet, April 21, 2005, at: www.innocentive.com/about/media/20050421_Talent247.pdf

9. Taylor, "Here's an Idea."

10. Ibid.

11. http://www.who.int/mediacentre/news/releases/2003/pr31/en/

12. See http://www.nyas.columbia.edu/sars/ for more about this collaboration.

13. Doug Beizer, "IT as a Health Care Warrior," *Washington Technology* 20, 22 (November 5, 2005), at: http://www.washingtontechnology.com/news/20_22/news/27365-1.html

14. Ibid.

CHAPTER 3

1. Isaac Asimov, *Prelude to Foundation* (New York: Doubleday, 1988).

2. Carl Hayden Bee Research Center, at: gears.tucson.ars.ag.gov

3. J. B. Berg et al., "Results from a Dozen Years of Election Futures Markets Research" (2001), at: http://www.biz.uiowa.edu/iem/archive/BFNR_2000.pdf

4. William C. Taylor, "Here's an Idea: Let Everyone Have Ideas," *New York Times*, Sunday Business, March 26, 2006, p. Bu-3.

5. Business Innovation Factory BIF-1: Stories of Innovation. "Jim Lavoie: Creatively Inspiring Employees as Sources of Innovation," at: http://www.businessinnovationfactory.com/index.php?option=com_content&task=view&id=185&Itemid=109

6. Ibid.

7. www.rite-solutions.com

8. Taylor, "Here's an Idea."

9. Ornit Raz, "Social Versus Geographical Influences on Organizational Strategy in Israeli Software Companies: Isomorphism in Action," M.Sc. thesis, Technion, Institute of Technology, Haifa, 2001.

10. AnnaLee Saxenian, *Regional Advantage: Culture and Competition in Silicon Valley and Route* 128 (Cambridge: Harvard University Press, 2000).

11. David Liben-Nowell and Jon Kleinberg, "The Link Prediction Problem for Social Networks," *Proceedings of the Twelfth Annual ACM International Conference on Information and Knowledge Management*, ACM Press (2003): 556-559.

12. Lada A. Adamic and Eytan Adar, "Friends and Neighbors on the Web," *Social Networks* 25, 3 (2003): 211-230.

13. Leo Katz, "A New Status Index Derived from Sociometric Analysis," *Psychometrika* 18, 1 (1953): 39-43.

CHAPTER 4

1. *The Autobiography of Benjamin Franklin*, Chapter 8. Full text at: http://www.earlyamerica.com/lives/franklin/

2. Marie Boas Hall, "The Royal Society's Role in the Diffusion of Information in the Seventeenth Century," *Notes and Records of the Royal Society of London* 29, 2 (March 1975).

3. Ibid.

4. An *infinitesimal* is an arbitrarily small quantity—a number that is greater than absolute zero yet smaller than any positive real number. Early mathematicians, lacking a proper theory of limits, found it necessary to incorporate infinitesimals into their theories.

5. A transcript of the interview is at: http://www.ics.uci.edu/~ejw/csr/ nelson_pg.html, and the audio version is at: http://www.ics.uci.edu/~ejw/ csr/cyber.html

6. Karl von Frisch, "Die Tänze der Bienen" ("The Bees' Dances"), Österreichische Zoologische Zeitschrift 1 (1946): 1-48; Karl von Frisch, *The Dance Language and Orientation of Bees* (Cambridge, Mass.: Harvard University Press, 1967).

7. Mark Granovetter, "The Strength of Weak Ties," *American Journal of Sociology* 78, 6 (May 1973).

CHAPTER 5

1. Quoted in Thomas L. Friedman, *The World Is Flat: A Brief History of the Twenty-first Century* (New York: Farrar, Straus and Giroux, 2005), p. 231.

2. Gretchen Vogel, "A Day in the Life of a Topflight Lab," *Science*, September 3, 1999, at: http://www.sciencemag.org/cgi/content/full/285/5433/1531

3. *The Autobiography of Benjamin Franklin* (emphasis in original).

4. http://www.catb.org/~esr/writings/cathedral-bazaar/cathedral-bazaar/ ar01s07.html

5. Piero Scaruffi, *A History of Rock Music*, online at: http://www.scaruffi.com/vol1/mayall.html

6. In the recording industry, the term "artists and repertoire" (A&R) refers to the department and people responsible for scouting and developing talent.

7. Clifford Carlsen, "Jim Clark: 'Serial Entrepreneur' Still at It," *Silicon Valley/San Jose Business Journal*, July 9, 1999, at: http://sanjose.bizjournals.com/ sanjose/stories/1999/07/12/story4.html

8. John Markoff, "A Free and Simple Computer Link," *New York Times*, December 8, 1993.

9. Mark Pesce, "A Brief History of Cyberspace," ZDNet, October 15, 1995.

10. Later, the University of Illinois forced the company to change its name to Netscape Communications Corp.

11. The in-house name for the browser under development was "Mozilla"— a play on Godzilla and dubbed the "Mosaic Killer." The Mozilla name survives today in the Mozilla Foundation, a nonprofit organization that supports and provides leadership for the open-source Mozilla project, which has resulted in the popular open-source Firefox Web browser (which we discuss in a bit more detail in Chapter 11).

12. Quoted in Robert H. Reid, *Architects of the Web: 1,000 Days That Built the Future of Business* (New York: John Wiley and Sons, 1997).

13. Lydia Lee, "Boo hoo!," *Salon*, May 18, 2000, at: http://archive.salon. com/tech/log/2000/05/18/boo

14. Tristan Louis, "Boo.com Goes Bust," May 19, 2000, at: http://www.tnl.net/ blog/engry/Boo.com_Goes_Bust

CHAPTER 6

1. Charles MacKay, *Extraordinary Popular Delusions and the Madness of Crowds*, 1841.

2. The idea for including Albania came to Scott based on work he did assisting the author of a book on a completely different topic than the current text, but in which the Albanian pyramid scheme is mentioned. See Elena Panaritis, *Prosperity Unbound: Property Rights, Informality and Tapping the Potential of Markets under Stress* (Hampshire, England: Palgrave Macmillan, 2006).

3. en.wikipedia.org/wiki/Webvan

4. Miguel Helft, "What a Long, Strange Trip It's Been for Webvan," *The Industry Standard*, July 23, 2001, at: http://www.thestandard.com/article/ 0,1902,27911,00.html

5. Warren E. Leary, "Better Communication Is NASA's Next Frontier," *New York Times*, April 14, 2004, p. A-24.

6. Matthew L. Wald, "Management Issues Looming in Inquiry on Shuttle Safety," *New York Times*, August 6, 2003, p. A-11.

7. Matthew L. Wald and John Schwartz, "Shuttle Inquiry Uncovers Flaws in Communication," *New York Times*, August 14, 2003, p. A-9.

8. Ibid.

9. In Todd Halvorson, "O'Keefe to Start Changes at Top: Behavioral Scientists Aim to Help NASA Fix 'Broken Safety Culture'," *Florida Today*, April 14, 2004.

10. Quoted in Bethany MacLean and Peter Elkind, *The Smartest Guys in the Room: The Amazing Rise and Scandalous Fall of Enron* (New York: Portfolio, 2003).

11. Ibid.

12. Fortune, November 1, 1993.

13. Our description of The Family draws heavily on a thorough analysis by sociologists Gordon and Gary Shepherd. See G. Shepherd and G. Shepherd, "The Family in Transition: The Moral Career of a New Religious Movement," 2002 CESNUR Conference, Salt Lake City, June 25, 2002. Quoted with permission of Gary Shepherd.

14. *New Testament* (King James Version), Romans 2:ll: "For there is no respect of persons with God."

15. http://en.wikipedia.org/wiki/Children_of_God

16. http://www.religionnewsblog.com/9922

17. Isaac Asimov, "Of What Use?" (1973), in Asimov, *The Beginning and the End* (New York: Doubleday, 1977).

CHAPTER 7

1. In Eric McLuhan and Frank Zingrone (eds.), *Essential McLuhan* (Oxford, England: Routledge, 1997), p. 283.

2. Dave Sifry, "State of the Blogosphere, April 2006. Part 1: On Blogosphere Growth," at: http://technorati.com/weblog/blogosphere

3. http://billives.typepad.com/portals_and_km

4. www.memeorandum.com

5. www.digg.com

6. Richard Dawkins, *The Selfish Gene* (New York: Oxford University Press, 1976). Although a neologism, the word "meme" likely comes from the Greek word for "memory."

7. www.scripting.com

8. http://www.scripting.com/2006/03/05.html

9. http://reality.media.mit.edu

10. Ryan Singel, "When Cell Phones Become Oracles, *Wired News*, July 25, 2005, at: http://www.wired.com/news/technology/wireless/0,68263-0.html?tw= wn_story_page_prev2

11. Joshua Randall, "Real-time Lighting System for Large Group Interaction," May 2002, at: www.media.mit/edu/resenv/GiveawaySensors/auplighting-5.pdf

12. "Inexpensive 'Giveaway' Sensors for Large-Crowd Interaction," at: http://www.media.mit.edu/resenv/GiveawaySensors/index.html

13. "Handheld Transmitters Connect Students and Teachers in Class," *Duke Dialogue*, February 15, 2005, at: http://www.dukenews,duke.edu/news/ transmitters_0205.html

14. Rusty Miller, "Students Click Their Way Through Classes," Associated Press, July 4, 2005.

CHAPTER 8

1. http://www.insna.org/INSNA/na_inf.html

2. Internet Engineering Task Force (IETF), Network Working Group, Request for Comments: 1336, "Who's Who in the Internet," May 1992.

Clark was named in this document as one of two dozen people who had made the most significant contributions to making the Internet possible.

3. Betweenness centrality of a team describes how much the communication flow in a team is centralized. The larger betweenness centrality is, the more it is centralized by one person or a small subteam.

4. http://en.wikinews.org/wiki/Wikinews:Original_reporting

5. http://forum.ecoustics.com/bbs/messages

6. This study was done by Sung Joo Bae, an MIT doctoral student, and Sebastian Schnorf of Swisscom Innovation Research. It grew out of a class project in Peter's course at MIT.

7. http://www.cs.cmu.edu/~enron

8. "Enron Mastermind Pleads Guilty," at:
http://www.cbsnews.com/stories/2002/10/17/national/main526018.shtml

9. The study was initially done as a project in Peter's course (2005) by Marius Cramer, Daniel Oster, and Qinfang Li from the University of Cologne, along with Mousa Al-Mohammed from Helsinki University of Technology.

CHAPTER 9

1. Eric Hoffer, *The Ordeal of Change* (New York: Harper & Row, 1952).

2. TeCFlow is available for free download at: http://www.ickn.org/ickndemo

3. This was discovered by course members Sebastian Schiefer, Lutz Tegethoff, and Ilkka Lyytinen.

4. The topics are Wikinews, how the course was measured, and an analysis of the ISIWeb database.

CHAPTER 10

1. *Hamlet*, Act IV, Scene 5.

2. Jenny Wohlfarth, "House Blend," October 2004, at:
http://www.howdesign. com/db/features/starbucks.asp

3. U.S. Patent and Trademark Office, "USPTO Releases Annual List of Top 10 Organizations Receiving Most U.S. Patents," January 10, 2006, at:
http://www.uspto.gov/web/offices/com/speeches/06-03.htm

4. The Open Source Initiative definition sets out specific conditions that go well beyond availability of source code. The definition can be read at:
http://www.opensource.org/docs/definition.php

5. "IBM to give away 500 patents: Move marks major shift of intellectual-property strategy," Reuters, January 11, 2005, at:
http://www.msnbc.msn.com/ id/6811975

6. Jena McGregor, "The World's Most Innovative Companies," *Business Week*, April 24, 2006, p. 66.

7. Larry Huston and Nabil Sakkab, "Connect and Develop: Inside Procter & Gamble's New Model for Innovation," *Harvard Business Review*, March 2006. The authors are P&G vice president for innovation and knowledge and senior vice president for corporate R&D, respectively.

8. Telephone interview with the authors, March 6, 2006.

9. http://newsroom.cisco.com/dlls/tln/exec_team/chambers/chambers_vision.html

10. Richard Siklos, "Death by Smiley Face: When Rivals Disdain Profit," *New York Times*, April 2, 2006, p. BU-3.

11. As we mentioned in Chapter 4, Dr. Vannevar Bush—then the science advisor to President Franklin Roosevelt—proposed the idea of "Memex" (the precursor to the concept of hypertext) in a July 1945 article in *The Atlantic Monthly* titled "As We May Think."

12. Major Dale J. Long, USAF (Ret.), "A Brief History of Personal Computing Part IV: 'How the Web Was Won'," CHIPS—*The Department of the Navy Information Technology Magazine*, Spring 2003, at: http://www.chips.navy.mil/archives/03_spring/webpages/DaleSpring2003.htm

13. CERN is the common name for the European Organization for Nuclear Research, which is the world's largest particle physics laboratory. Situated just west of Geneva on the border between France and Switzerland, it is considered the birthplace of the World Wide Web. Tim Berners-Lee, who we mention briefly in Chapter 4, worked at CERN when he initiated the ENQUIRE project that became the World Wide Web.

14. Clayton M. Christensen, *The Innovators Dilemma: When New Technologies Cause Great Firms to Fail* (Cambridge, Mass.: Harvard Business School Press, 1997).

15. Telephone interview with the authors, March 6, 2006.

16. Eduardo Porter, "Auto Bailout Seems Unlikely," *New York Times*, April 14, 2006.

17. Mark Ward, "BT Claims Patent on Web Links," BBC News, June 20, 2000, at: http://news.bbc.co.uk/1/hi/sci/tech/798475.stm. See also the Wikipedia entry at: http://en.wikipedia.org/wiki/BT_Group_plc